Married to the Wind

by Wayne Lynch

Whitecap Books

North Vancouver • British Columbia • Canada

Canadian Cataloguing in Publication Data

Lynch, Wayne.
Married to the Wind

Includes index.
Bibliography: p.
ISBN 0-920620-52-3

C.I.P./ISBN Data
1. Prairies — North America. 2. Prairie ecology —
North America. 3. Grassland ecology — North
America. 4. Habitat (Ecology) I. Title.
QH541.5.P7L96 1984 574.5'2643'097 C84-091259-5

Designed by Michael E. Burch
Printed by D. W. Friesen & Sons Ltd.
Altona, Manitoba

© Whitecap Books Ltd.
1086 W. 3rd Avenue
North Vancouver, B.C., Canada

First Edition 1984

Printed in Canada

To Aubrey

I have known no finer companion.

Contents

Foreword

I came to the prairies in the early part of this century. For one whose roots were deep on the east coast, my first contact with the wide open prairies was a thrilling and enlightening one. It was not the sombre picture some authors had described. As I descended from the train, I viewed a magical, sparkling vista, a great sweep of country that seemed to stretch to the world's end.

I recall, later in the spring when the snow had melted, the "grass cover shook in the sun for leagues and leagues on either hand." And the air above? Perfumed with roses and wolf willow, while purple patches of crocuses and yellow splashes of golden bean reflected the brilliant sunshine. Since that first year, life on the grasslands has presented me with an insistent call, a powerful and moving influence.

John Milton said that a good book is the precious lifeblood of a master spirit. Such a book is *Married to the Wind*, in which a great area of our plains is sensitively portrayed.

Dr. Wayne Lynch has made a major contribution to the understanding and appreciation of the Canadian grasslands, a vital component of our natural heritage. In an authoritative and most readable text, permeated with the out-of-doors, the lifelong naturalist succeeds in capturing the distinctive mood and colour of the horizontal world that reaches to the rim of the sky. In bright, perceptive writing the author gives valuable insight and deep knowledge of the land for which he has an abiding love.

In the grasslands, where the author stretched his eyes and his soul, he discovered as Fabré did a century ago the whole of a universe. He discovered the hidden glory of common things, "the colours in everyday earth, the humblest flower's birth."

Information so gleaned expands the awareness of readers and is a tribute to the beauty, the grandeur and the mystery of the prairie environment. And to its loneliness.

Married to the Wind is a superb book, perfectly controlled, with accurate observations most interestingly written and illustrated.

Elizabeth R. Cruickshank

Introduction

Cradled between the foothills of the Rocky Mountains and the forested uplands of the Canadian Shield is an expanse of land open to discovery. Here there is just enough openness, just enough flatness, space and distance, and just enough uncertainty to rouse the spirit. Here, there is room to stretch the imagination. It is a land of life, and a land of harsh reality, enticing in its endless moods. It is a place where the amber glow of twilight throws the naked hills into soft relief, and where the plaintive call of the curlew drifts from all around. And it is a place where the wind and the pungent smell of pasture sage evoke memories from our unseen past. These are the grasslands.

Grasses have figured prominently in the history of man. They nurtured the earliest civilizations that flanked the Tigris, the Euphrates, the Nile and the Yellow Rivers. At that time, 40% of the earth's land surface was cloaked in grass, but the steady encroachment of man, his cattle, and his plow has reduced that by half. Still, grasses have the widest distribution of any flowering plant on earth, and grasses of one kind or another can be found on every continent. In South America the grasslands are called pampas and llanos, those of Eurasia and Africa are called steppes and veldts respectively, and in North America the vast grassy expanses are called plains and prairies. Of all of the world's grasslands, the quintessential grassland is that which occupies the heart of North America. In its day the North American plains supported the largest number of grazing animals the earth has ever known: 60 million bison, 40 million pronghorn and millions of elk and mule deer. Today, though vastly reduced, the grasslands of North America are still premier.

To the casual observer grass is grass. But within a square meter of grassland there may exist as much variety and complexity as within a hectare of forest. Thus, the North American grassland region is not a vast uniform sea of grass, but a mosaic of grassland communities which differ in their vegetation and wildlife. Within Canada, the regional climate, soil, and topography has subdivided the grasslands into three separate prairie communities: the tallgrass prairie, the fescue prairie, and the mixed grass prairie. (Fig. 1)

The tallgrass prairie, also called the true prairie, occupies the eastern margin of Canada's grasslands, and is situated in south-central Manitoba.

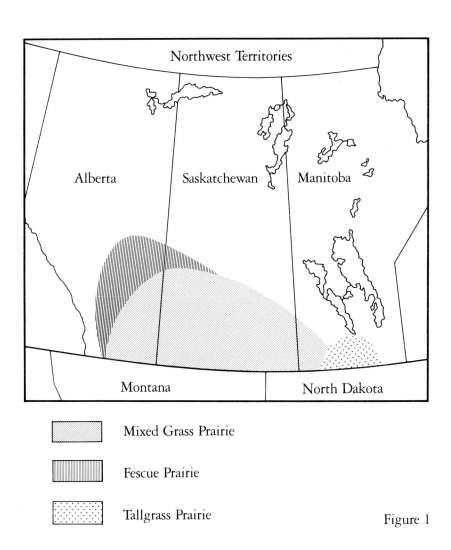

Mixed Grass Prairie

Fescue Prairie

Tallgrass Prairie

Figure 1

The tallgrass prairie extends as far south as Texas, and throughout its length it occupies a position between the deciduous forest in the east and the mixed grass prairie in the west. The fertility of the tallgrass prairie spelled its demise, and most of it is now buried under wheat and corn. The second prairie community, the fescue prairie, forms the northern and western boundary of Canada's grasslands. The fescue prairie is found in both Saskatchewan and Alberta, and it derives its name from the predominance of the grass, rough fescue. In the centre of the Canadian grasslands is the mixed grass prairie. It is the largest of Canada's three grassland communities and the most extensive grassland region in North America. The mixed grass prairie extends for 2000 kilometers from Canada to Texas, consuming the lion's share of the Central Plains of North America. Within Canada, the extent of the mixed grass prairie can most easily be remembered by visualizing a triangle, the base of which runs along the international border from the foothills of the Rocky Mountains to a point just east of the border between Saskatchewan and Manitoba. The apex of the triangle is located 350 kilometers north, along the Alberta-Saskatchewan border.

The Canadian mixed grass prairie is the subject of this book. However, much of what I will discuss about the mixed grass prairie also applies to the fescue and tallgrass prairies, and to the contiguous mixed grassland regions of the northern United States, as vegetation and wildlife habitually ignore political boundaries, and frequently defy the scientific limits we set for them.

Within any ecosystem there are subdivisions called *habitats*. Canada's mixed grass prairie ecosystem is composed of five habitats: flat to gently rolling grassland plains; sandhill areas; wooded valleys called coulees; badlands; and sloughs, the regional term for ponds and potholes. Each habitat will be covered in a separate chapter.

The animals in each habitat may be herbivores (plant eaters), carnivores (meat eaters) or scavengers; in other words, each animal has its own *niche*, or strategy for sustaining itself. Generally, no two species occupy the same niche in a habitat

and commonly they complement each other. A good example of this is the large herbivores of the grasslands. At first, the bison, mule deer and pronghorn appear to compete for the same niche. On closer observation we see that the bison is primarily a grazer and prefers to crop grass and sedges. The mule deer is more of a browser and favours the leaves and buds of shrubs like snowberry, saskatoon and chokecherry. The pronghorn is both a browser and a grazer, but is content with less palatable forage, such as, cactus, juniper and sagebrush. In another instance, when food sources are identical, species may hunt at different times of the day to avoid competition. The red-tailed hawk and the great horned owl both prey on the varying hare, but the owl hunts at night and the hawk hunts during the day. Some species fill several niches and live in more than one habitat. For example, the coyote may feed on plants, animals or carrion, and it may hunt or forage in all five of the mixed grassland habitats. These different ways that a habitat is partitioned permit more complete use of available space and food, and encourage the greatest possible diversity of wildlife.

In the grasslands and elsewhere, plant and animal distribution is not random. Plants and animals inhabit a particular ecosystem, whether it be the grasslands, tundra, desert, or forest, because they have certain characteristics or adaptations. The prickly pear cactus grows readily in the drier regions of the mixed grasslands because it happens to have certain structural features that result in low water losses, and thus low water requirements. Charles Darwin was the first to elucidate the theory of evolution by natural selection over a century ago. Central to Darwin's theory are several observations. The first is that creatures produce large numbers of offspring, frequently far in excess of the number that will survive to become breeding adults. For example, a single wood tick may lay 8000 eggs. Darwin also noted that offspring varied. From this he reasoned that over millions of years the number of variations in offspring is astronomical. From the many varieties, the environment selects those that are best suited to survive the prevailing conditions. The survivors leave offspring, thus perpetuating their particular variation. Evolution is primarily a process of selection by the environment. As the world evolved, environments changed and the criteria for survival changed. At every step, the existing environment selected (and still does) from among the available variations, those that were best suited for that environment. Knowing this we can postulate how some creatures became extinct. When the environment changed too quickly there was insufficient time for successful random variation to arise. These creatures, being unable to dictate the direction of desirable traits, were left to wait for chance genetic change that never came, and the environment passed them by. Thus, in the grassland ecosystem, each and every plant, insect, bird, reptile and mammal has been selected because of its unique set of characteristics that make it best suited for that environment.

The earliest travellers to the prairies came from Europe and the wooded regions of eastern Canada, and they frequently described the prairies in terms of deficiency. The pioneers that followed them were no more insightful; they viewed the prairies as an adversary, to be conquered, controlled and subdued. They set forth to "tame the West," and "break the land." The "sodbusters" were proud, and so they should be, for in less than a century they plowed under two-thirds of the nation's native prairie to assuage the appetite of agriculture. It is an appetite that has not slackened, and every year another 40,000 hectares is offered up. Man can be brilliantly destructive when he puts his mind to it, and his record with the grasslands attests to that. If we were to chronicle the history of the earth in a book of 1000 pages, each page would cover 4½ million years. Grasses first appear 15 pages from the end. In the final 5 pages the Central Plains of North America become drier and the grasses spread to form a prairie. Then comes man; his migration from Asia and his occupation of the Americas are crammed into the last word of the book. Somehow, the 17th century arrival of the Europeans, the wholesale slaughter of the bison, the decimation of the Plains Indian culture, the extermination of the swift fox, prairie wolf and grizzly, and the destruction of 24,000,000 hectares of native Canadian prairie are telescoped into the final period.

Our capacity to manipulate the environment has lulled many of us into the belief that we are somehow divorced from the natural community, and not subject to its laws. Our calm disregard for the limits of nature, and our frequent refusal to accept the universality of natural laws, by which both we and the natural community are governed, may eventually seal the fate of the environment, and ultimately our own fate.

For decades conservationists have begged for the recognition of the intangible worth of wilderness: scientific, ecological, and esthetic. Each time we allow an organism to disappear we lose more than genetic diversity, we lose some of our humanity. But, until we know what we have, we do not know what we can lose. To understand the grasslands is to know their worth. In the pages that follow I welcome you to discover the excitement, the diversity, the intricacy, and the beauty of Canada's mixed grass prairie. In addition, I hope to transmit a concern for one of the integral components of our nation. To allow the grasslands to disappear would be to sacrifice a landscape that raises the quality of life above mere survival.

The Land — Its Face and Its Temperament

Above and within the earth are the fires that shape our world. Above, the sun seethes at several million °C and determines our global climate through the agents of wind, rain and temperature. Beneath us, the molten interior of the earth simmers at 4000°C. Heat from this inner fire leaks to the surface and fractures the earth's crust into pieces, called tectonic plates, and then shifts the plates about. For billions of years both fires have burned, and for billions of years they have influenced the prairie region.

Drifting Continents and Spreading Oceans

The term *plate tectonics* is used to describe the dual phenomena of moving continents, or continental drift, and sea floor spreading. Starting in the late 1960's, the elaboration of these two phenomena revolutionized the sciences of geology, geophysics, paleontology and many others. Overnight, scientists could explain similarities in fossils found on different continents that are separated by thousands of kilometers of open ocean. An understanding of plate tectonics helps to explain a number of features of the mixed grass prairie region that are evident today. Prairie coal and petroleum, for example, originated as deposits in tropical seas when North America straddled more southern latitudes. In another instance, the occurrence of thousands of dinosaur fossils in southern Alberta can be explained.

Dinosaurs were reptiles that needed a year-round tropical climate. They could never have survived today's frigid winter temperatures, so that either the global climate has changed drastically, or the Alberta region was at one time farther south. The former explanation is widely discounted, and the latter one has wide support. Plate tectonics also explains the global distribution of volcanoes and earthquakes, and the mechanisms of mountain building. Though none of these events directly befall the prairies the reasons for their absence is an interesting part of the story.

Central to the theory of plate tectonics is the notion that the crust of the earth, rather than being a continuous layer of rock, is fragmented by heat from the earth's interior into at least 6 major plates and as many minor plates. North America is part of the massive Americas plate which carries both the North American and South American continents. In the Canadian region of the Americas plate the western edge of the plate coincides with the Pacific edge of British Columbia, while the eastern edge of the plate extends to the middle of the Atlantic Ocean, 3000 kilometers east of Newfoundland. Thus the boundaries of plates do not necessarily coincide with the boundaries of the continents, and most of the plates include both continental and ocean floor crustal sections. The other major tectonic plates are Eurasia, Africa, India, Antarctica and the Pacific.

The plates are in continual motion, shifting and jostling for position. Since they are relatively rigid, all of the action occurs along their edges at the boundaries between adjacent plates. Plates really only do three things: move apart, collide, or slide past each other.

Running down the center of the floor of the Atlantic Ocean is a ridge of mountains, part of a 59,000 kilometer ridge system that meanders through the Atlantic, Pacific, and Indian Oceans like the seam on a baseball. This oceanic ridge system is an area of sea floor spreading, where adjacent tectonic plates are moving apart. Along the ridge, molten rock from the underlying mantle of the earth wells up, cools and hardens, and is welded to the edges of the ocean plate on either side of the rift. The newly formed ocean crust then moves away in a continual conveyor belt fashion. It is no coincidence that the ridge in the Atlantic is equidistant from the eastern coast of Canada and the western coast of North Africa. These lands were once joined, but 200 million years ago an area of spreading developed between them and has been rafting them apart ever since. At the present rate of ocean floor spreading, Canada will move west, in your lifetime, a distance roughly equivalent to your height.

If new crust is continually being formed at the oceanic ridge system then there must be an area where crust is being consumed, or else the earth would gradually increase in diameter. Zones of consumption, called *subduction zones,* occur where tectonic plates collide and form a system of deep ocean trenches. The entire western edge of the Pacific plate, running through the islands of Japan, the Philippines, and New Zealand, is a subduction zone where the Pacific plate collides with the Eurasian plate. When the lighter crust of the continental Eurasian plate collides with the denser crust of the Pacific plate, the denser oceanic crust slips beneath. As it dips into the trench, it folds, fractures, and eventually melts and is absorbed into the mantle. Earthquakes and volcanoes are the surface manifestations of this crustal digestive process, which explains the frequency of such phenomena along the western Pacific. The impact of colliding may also thrust the crust up into mountains. Eighty million years ago there was a subduction zone along the western coast of Canada. The oceanic Pacific plate plunged beneath the continental Americas plate, and, over millions of years, thrust up the Rocky Mountains. The formation of the Rocky Mountains was a monumental event for the Central Plains. Without the shielding effect of the mountains the plains would not have become as warm or arid, and the grasslands would never have developed. Weather systems coming from the Pacific must rise to clear the mountains. As they do, the air is cooled and heavy rains result, so that the air reaching the mixed grass prairie on the leeward side of the mountains has been robbed of its moisture and has relatively little precipitation to surrender to the prairie, a phenomena called the rain shadow effect.

Finally, the third pattern of tectonic plate movement occurs when plates move parallel to each other. The movement of the plates is not smooth and regular along its edges, and the plates frequently stick. In this area, pressure builds until it is sufficient to overcome the resistance and the plates jump back into position. The result is an earthquake. Along the western coast of the United States the Pacific plate and the Americas plate are sliding past each other. The San Andreas fault in California marks the junction between these plates and is a notorious earthquake zone.

Continents and oceans have repeatedly been fractured, repositioned, and rafted around the globe throughout the earth's 4.5 billion year history. Climatic conditions on earlier continents differed considerably from today because of differences in the size of the continents, the pattern of ocean currents, and most of all because of changes in the latitudinal position of the continents on the globe. Following the mixed grass prairie region in its course over the last 600 million years can tell us much about what we see today.

The Primeval Plains

Six hundred million years ago life existed only in the oceans of the earth. The land itself was barren, lifeless rock. The atmosphere contained little oxygen and large amounts of carbon dioxide, methane and ammonium. Lethal ultraviolet rays were just beginning to interact with oxygen to form a protective layer of ozone in the upper atmosphere. The area that was to be Canada's prairie region straddled the equator, and lingered there for over 100 million years. During this time the land was repeatedly inundated by warm shallow seas, and sediments slowly accumulated at the bottom of these seas. The mixture of rock sediments and sea animal skeletons, compressed over time, created beds of limestone and dolomite. These beds of limestone and dolomite (buried thousands of meters deep) underlie most of the present day mixed grass prairie, and are exposed only in the northern parts of the prairie provinces. Slabs of these ancient rocks, rich in fossil corals and snails, were used to construct the Natural History Museum, the Legislative Building and University buildings in Regina, Saskatchewan.

In the next phase of its journey, the prairie region moved farther south. Globally, this was a time of great importance, when the first creatures, the ancestors of the scorpions, crawled out of the sea and dared to challenge the land. Plants also made their debut on land, and atmospheric oxygen levels gradually rose as a byproduct of photosynthesis.

During the following period, called the Devonian Period (Fig. 2), the prairie region was driven still farther south, and occupied latitudes similar to those of present day northern Argentina. Cradled between 20°S and 40°S latitude, the plains were hot and dry. There were reefs along the edge of the exposed land. The shallow coastal seas, with their tidal flats and lagoons, were subject to high rates of evaporation which concentrated and precipitated salts into beds of sediments. Today we recognize these sediments as deposits of potassium chloride, commonly called potash. More than 50% of the world's known reserves of potash are located in the mixed grass prairie region of Saskatchewan.

The Devonian Period continued the evolutionary trends inherited from the preceding periods. As new environments opened up, opportunities for new forms of life arose. The Devonian Period witnessed the emergence of primitive fish from the sea onto land, starting the invasion and colonization of the land by vertebrates. From these fish evolved amphibians, reptiles, mammals and eventually the human race.

During the succeeding 65 million years in the Carboniferous Period the plains retraced their route and returned to equatorial latitudes, and in the wake of the Carboniferous Period all the continents of the world, including North America, were driven together by the processes of plate tectonics, forming a supercontinent called Pangea. Amphibians were the dominant land animals at this time, but reptiles had become well established; they were poised to take supremacy in the "Age of the Dinosaurs."

The Origins of Petroleum and Coal

The supercontinent, Pangea, started to break up about 200 million years ago. The prairie region, along with the rest of North America, was ferried north out of the tropics as the nascent Atlantic Ocean widened under the action of sea floor spreading. En route, the interior plains of North America were again inundated by the sea, this time accumulating deposits of small marine organisms, both plants and animals. The decomposition of such marine organisms produces

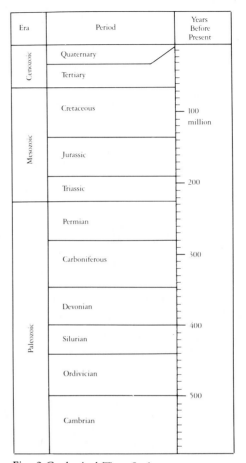

Era	Period	Years Before Present
Cenozoic	Quaternary	
	Tertiary	
Mesozoic	Cretaceous	100 million
	Jurassic	
	Triassic	200
Paleozoic	Permian	
	Carboniferous	300
	Devonian	400
	Silurian	
	Ordivician	500
	Cambrian	

Fig. 2 Geological Time Scale

petroleum. When rock sediments, which were simultaneously accumulating on the ocean floor, became compacted with time into rocks, the petroleum-forming organisms were either trapped in fine-grained rocks and formed oil shales, or they were squeezed into coarser, more porous rocks that acted as reservoirs. Natural gas (methane) settled above the oil.

The Cretaceous Period was the last period in the "Age of the Dinosaurs," and it ended with the disappearance of these reptilian behemoths whose fossils are found throughout the prairies. The geological sequelae of the Cretaceous Period (65-13 million years ago) are readily visible in the mixed grass prairie. In addition, large amounts of sediments, sometimes 1000 meters thick, settled out on the bottoms of Cretaceous seas, forming the bedrock that surfaces everywhere in the prairies. Finally, the Cretaceous Period left the prairies with important reserves of coal.

The climate on the Canadian plains region during the Cretaceous Period was warm and genial, similar to the present climate of Florida. The vegetation was lush, with rich stands of redwoods, palms, ferns, horsetails and gingkos. In many areas, as trees died they fell into loose boggy soil and shallow pools of stagnant water where the concentration of oxygen was low. The low oxygen concentration in the water discouraged the growth of bacteria, and thus decay, so that the vegetation was incompletely broken down. The black mass of partially decomposed muck, called *peat*, was the first stage in the formation of coal. As more trees died and the sediments piled up, the underlying peat became compressed, squeezing out the oxygen and water, resulting in an increase in the percentage of carbon and producing *lignite*, the next grade of coal. Further compaction produced a further increase in the percentage of carbon and transformed the lignite into a higher grade of coal, called *bituminous coal*. Finally, if the bituminous coal was subjected to still greater pressure, it was metamorphosed into *anthracite*, the highest grade of coal, with a carbon content of 90%. Generally, the higher the carbon content the better the coal is as a fuel. The higher grades of coal are usually found at greater depths, and are expensive to extract. Seams of bituminous coal are found in the mixed grass prairie of Alberta.

Close to the end of the Cretaceous Period the prairie region moved into temperate latitudes which were much the same as today. In the following 12 million years more coal was formed, this time from forests of cypress, cedar, magnolia and chestnut; these latter coal beds are the lignite deposits found in southern Saskatchewan and southwestern Manitoba.

After the Dinosaurs

The dinosaurs suddenly disappeared 65 million years ago. By that time the Rocky Mountains were partially formed. During this period, the Tertiary Period, the prairie region was never again flooded by the sea, because of a general uplift of the continent that has persisted until today. Thus the bare land was left to erode. In the ensuing millenia, sediments were eroded and washed down from the newly formed mountains in the west and spread across the prairies. The debris was swept as far east as Manitoba, but it never acquired the great depths, nor the extensive coverage, of the deposits of the preceding Cretaceous Period.

With the abrupt disappearance of the dinosaurs, numerous ecological vacancies arose. With little or no competition, mammals responded to the vacancies with a rapid expansion of species. The Tertiary Period witnessed the rise of the mammals to dominance, a dominance that still persists. Mammals, with their high, constant body temperature, could be active in all climates, in all seasons, and at any hour of the day. This was in sharp contrast to the previously reigning reptiles which had been seriously restricted in their mobility by their dependence on the heat energy of the sun. Mammals also provided their offspring with special care, a characteristic which was virtually nonexistent in the reptiles. The mammals gave their young milk, grooming, protection and instruction, all of which increased the likelihood of survival. Natural selection had chosen again, and the mammals were the winners.

Three Prairie Levels

In the last 600 million years the plains have been repeatedly shifted, flooded, dumped on and scoured by erosion. The present bedrock topography of the prairies is the legacy of those years, and for such a complex history the visible sequelae exhibit a simple pattern. The bedrock of the Canadian plains lies in three levels, or steps, with the lowest level in the east, and the highest in the west.

The Alberta Plains are highlands of gently rolling and hummocky terrain, and they are not only the highest (600-1200 m) but also the widest of the three prairie levels. They extend from the foothills of the Rocky Mountains to the escarpment of the Missouri Coteau in mid-Saskatchewan. The Missouri Coteau is actually a chain of hills that enter Saskatchewan from the United States, just west of Estevan, and run northwest to the South Saskatchewan River. The hills bear simple but explicit names: Tit, Cactus, the Dirt Hills — names that suited pioneers with a penchant for utility, not poetry.

East of the Coteau are the Saskatchewan Plains, the second prairie level, but the transition is unlikely to be noticed by a traveller along the Trans-Canada Highway. The Saskatchewan Plains are 400 kilometers wide, stretching into Manitoba, and they vary in elevation from 300-600 meters. The eastern boundary of the Saskatchewan Plains is the Manitoba Escarpment. This escarpment, like the Missouri Coteau, has been cut by rivers into separate hill formations. Near Brandon, Manitoba, the Trans-Canada Highway passes through the widest cut, occupied by the Assiniboine River. The string of hills that marks the Manitoba Escarpment also runs northwest, and parallels those of the Missouri Coteau, but they are much higher and have earned the right to be called mountains: Turtle, Riding, Duck, and Porcupine mountains. Also, since these mountains skirt the eastern boundary of the mixed grass prairie where there is more rainfall, they are often heavily wooded in aspen, birch, and conifers, whereas the hills of the Missouri Coteau are covered with grass.

East of the Manitoba Escarpment are the Manitoba Lowlands. They are the third and lowest of the three prairie levels, and they lie between the Manitoba Escarpment and the emergent granite uplands of the Canadian Shield. The Lowlands in the north are heavily wooded and dotted with lakes, but in the south they boast some of the most prosperous farmland in the west, and the only remnant of the tallgrass prairie in Canada. The southern Lowlands owe their fertility to a rich endowment of clays and silts left by Lake Agassiz, which formed in the wake of the melting glacier about 10,000 years ago.

Though the three prairie levels describe the basic arrangement of the prairie bedrock, and thus the gross features of the topography, it was the Ice Age that finally sculptured the fine features of the landscape, and left the prairies with the landforms that we see everywhere today.

The Ice Age

The present Ice Age probably started about 2 million years ago. Controversy exists about how often the ice advanced, what starts an Ice Age, and whether there will be another, but speculation, disagreement and controversy have always been integral elements of science, and part of its appeal.

Glaciers presently cover 10% of the earth's land surface, the bulk of it found in the ice caps of Greenland and Antarctica. During the height of the last glaciation nearly ⅓ of the earth's land surface was laden with ice. The glaciers grew when more snow fell in the winter than melted in summer. As the depth of snow increased the snow became compacted into ice. The deepest layers were subjected to the greatest pressures, and they began to flow. As the glaciers grew in height they exerted an influence on the regional weather. They began to behave like mountains. Storms, driven by the predominantly southwesterly winds, rose when they met the glacial mounts. As the air rose it cooled and released its moisture in the form of snow. In this way, the southern lip of the glaciers thickened while their northern edges thinned. The glaciers crept slowly south.

Several centres of glaciation —Keewatin, Ungava, and Baffin Island — probably merged to create the massive Laurentide Ice Sheet that engulfed the greater part of Canada. At its centre in Hudson Bay, the Laurentide Ice Sheet was four kilometers thick. In the southern prairies, however, the Ice Sheet was much thinner, and the glacier never extended much beyond the international border.

The Ice Age was not a protracted, uninterrupted occupation of the land, but a series of successive episodes in which the ice sheet grew and covered the land, and then melted and withdrew from the land, called *glacial* and *interglacial* periods respectively. We are now living in an interglacial period. Specialists generally agree that glaciers have descended upon the prairie region at least four times since the start of this present Ice Age. These four glacial advances, starting with the last and most recent one, are called the Wisconsin, Illinoian, Kansan and Nebraskan Glaciations. (The sequence can be easily remembered if you recall the frequently asked question: Will the Ice Keep North? The initial letter of each word will serve to jog your memory.) Each glacial advance tended to erase the handiwork of previous episodes, and in the prairies the visible glacial effects are primarily those of the Wisconsin Glaciation, which started its retreat between 15,000 and 18,000 years ago. By 12,000 years ago the mixed grass prairie region was free of ice.

Causes of Glaciation

Central to a discussion of glaciation is an explanation of its causes. Glaciers grow when the mean global temperature drops. A drop of only 3-4°C would have been all that was necessary to start the glaciers of northern Canada growing and moving. But the presence of an ice field in itself will cause the temperature to drop. The age old dilemma of which came first, the chicken or the egg, is immediately apparent. But a number of new findings in recent decades will undoubtedly be proven influential.

The recent Ice Age, which started 2 million years ago, is not the first to befall the earth. Major Ice Ages occurred 450 million years ago, and then again 300 million years ago. Alfred Wegener, the scientific heretic who, sixty years ago, dared to propose that continents drift, noted quite early that the occurrence of major Ice Ages coincided with the presence of continents in polar latitudes. For example, during the last Ice Age in the Carboniferous Period, some 300 million years ago, a large ice mass covered Antarctica, India, and parts of South America, Africa and Australia, when these continents were clustered over southern polar latitudes. Currently two-thirds of the earth's land mass rides north of the equator with clustering in the polar latitude. It is speculated that the presence of continents in polar latitudes reduces the effectiveness of ocean circulation in distributing warm tropical currents to polar regions, and consequently leads to an overall reduction in global temperatures.

There are other factors which influence global temperatures. The amount of surface ice and snow on the earth determines the amount of solar reflection or absorption, and thus has an influence on world temperatures. Another factor may be volcanic ash spewed into the atmosphere, which intercepts the sun's rays and thus may lower the temperature of the earth. Still another proposal is that the sun's radiation output fluctuates, and even a minor variation of 1-2% would cool the earth. Finally, it is known that the earth's orbit about the sun is not constant, and that it undergoes periodic predictable variations. Though no one doubts that this occurs, many disagree as to the magnitude of its effect on global temperature.

In the final analysis the causes of glaciation are undoubtedly many, acting in consort. Though all of the factors mentioned may be involved, the latitudinal position of the continents seems to be the first prerequisite for the development of an Ice Age. The last Ice Age in the Carboniferous Period lasted for at least 50 million years until the continents shifted and moved towards the equator. This being the case, it appears that we are locked into another Ice Age, and we can expect glacial periods to recur repeatedly until the continents again drift to less polar latitudes.

Glaciers Shape the Prairie Landscape

Though the causes of the Ice Age are speculative the effects are not. The effects of the Ice Age fall into three simple categories: depositional, erosional, and sea level alteration. Each of these left its mark on the mixed grass prairie.

As the tongues of ice moved across the prairies they churned up fine and coarse rock which became imbedded in their undersurfaces. Additional rocks piled in front of the ice and along its sides as the glaciers pushed forward like highway graders forging a path. Within any given area the leading edge of the glacier was constantly shifting, with minor retreats and advances. When the glacier melted and withdrew, the rock it had nosed along was deposited as distinct mounds, called *end moraines*. Elsewhere, fragments of ice would break free, stagnate and melt, depositing their load of gravel and sand. At other times the receding glacier left a veneer of unsorted rocky rubble, the cargo it had carried in its undersurface. Across the breadth of the prairies these glacial events were repeated and erased innumerable times. When the ice left for the final time the bedrock of the plains was hidden, obscured beneath an uneven blanket of sand, silt, gravel and boulders, which was up to 150 meters thick. This irregular cover of glacial debris determined the final topography of the prairies and created the characteristic rolling terrain.

Glacial debris contains not only ground-up rocky material derived locally from the prairie Cretaceous bedrock, but also many large and small rocks plucked from the granite of the Canadian Shield by the glacier, and transported hundreds of kilometers south. These far-travelled rocks are called *erratics,* and they litter the prairies. Many erratics are quite large and served as scratching posts for the bison. In the treeless plains the boulders were a welcome occurrence, especially in spring when the shaggy beasts shed their heavy winter coats. Over the centuries the boulders were polished smooth, each in the centre of a hollow dug by thousands of hooves. The rubbing stones of the bison can still be spotted throughout the mixed grass prairie, haunting reminders of how we have changed the plains.

The normal drainage of the land in the three prairie levels is to the east and the north. As the glaciers melted they retreated in a northeasterly direction, forming a barrier to the normal drainage of the land, so that water was ponded between the glacier and the higher ground in the west. The ponded water formed glacial lakes that filled with sediments up to 6 meters thick. The flat, silt and clay bottoms of Rosetown, Indian Head, and Regina lakes were to become the prime wheat-growing areas of Saskatchean. The glacial lakes of Saskatchewan and Manitoba tended to spread out and cover large areas. Lake Agassiz, which formed in the Manitoba Lowlands, was the largest of all the glacial lakes and was probably the largest lake of any type that the earth has ever known. In Alberta, west of the Missouri Coteau, the land has greater relief; there the glacial lakes tended to be long and narrow, and occupied river valleys. The lakes were more transient than those of Saskatchewan and Manitoba and sediments had less time to accumulate. Typical glacial lakes in Alberta were the lakes near Lethbridge and Drumheller.

The meltwater that fed the glacial lakes spewed from the bottom of glaciers loaded with sand, gravel, silt and clay. The coarser material, sand and gravel, settled first into broad, fan-shaped outwash plains immediately adjacent to the glacier, while the finer silt and clay particles stayed suspended in the meltwater, and later settled in the glacial lakes. Today, the outwash plains form porous ground cover that often serves as underground reservoirs of water, called *aquifers.*

We have now covered the three different types of deposits found on the mixed grass prairie: those left by the glacier itself, those that formed on the bottoms of glacial lakes, and those spread by meltwater. By keeping in mind the fragment size of the deposits, and when and how the deposits accumulated, we can look at any fairly flat area in the mixed grass prairie and differentiate between a field of glacial debris, an old glacial lakebed, and an outwash plain. Deposits derived directly from the glacier itself are an unsorted jumble of rocky debris. This is the ground cover where erratics are most commonly found. This is also the most rolling of the three landscape deposits, and depressions are frequently occupied by sloughs. Glacial lakes form after a glacier has left an area, and their fine sediments of clays and silts mask any previous rocky deposits. Old lakebeds, then, have few visible rocks, are very level, and are frequently cultivated because of the high water-holding capacity of clay. Outwash plains, on the other hand, are composed of coarser sediments, often sand, deposited by flowing water. The water sorts the sediments so that the deposits are of uniform particle size. The porous nature of outwash plains normally precludes accumulation of surface water as sloughs, and makes them less attractive for agriculture.

In the erosional category of Ice Age effects, melting ice is again responsible. We have already seen that in the early phase of glacial departure from the prairies the ice blocked the normal northeast drainage route. Consequently, glacial meltwater, as well as the spillways of glacial lakes, coursed in a southerly direction and ultimately drained into the Mississippi River. The running water stripped away the glacial deposits and ate into the bedrock, carving out deep impressive valleys. The dramatic Milk River Valley, and the valleys of the Red Deer and Frenchman Rivers are examples of old meltwater channels. Today, these rivers are a shadow of their former size. The Frenchman River in southern Saskatchewan, for instance, is a mere 10 meters wide, but it flows along the bottom of a broad valley several kilometers wide in some areas, and 30-100 meters deep. In southern Alberta a whole series of dry-bottomed valleys etch the landscape. Whiskey Gap, Etzikom Coulee, Chin Coulee and Forty Mile Coulee are former meltwater channels created when the glacier relinquished its grip and withdrew from the land.

The Arrival of Man

Though the Ice Age is best known for its erosional and depositional effects on the landscape, the Ice Age affected the land in yet another way: it paved the way for the coming of man. With vast quantities of the earth's water imprisoned in ice, global sea levels dropped. A drop of 50 meters would have been all that was necessary to expose the submarine plateau spanning Alaska and Siberia. At the height of glaciation, however, global sea levels dropped more than 100 meters, creating an expansive land bridge 1500 kilometers wide between Asia and America. The migration began. Early man probably followed herds of game that also moved across the bridge from Siberia to Alaska. The immigrants included bison, deer, mammoths and mastodons, and with them their predators: sabre-tooth tigers, lions, bears, wolves and man. Camels and horses moved in the opposite direction, from Alaska to Siberia. It is uncertain how long man has been a North American, but estimates of 40,000 years are common. The earliest stone tools come from the Yukon and are 27,000 years old. But no matter when it was that man first arrived on the continent, his presence on the Canadian prairies 12,000 years ago is unquestionable. Then, migrating at an easy fifteen kilometers per year man might have reached Panama in only 600 years. Practically overnight, in the time scale of the earth, man moved from immigrant hunter to master of a continent.

Postglacial Forests

Early man in the Canadian mixed grass prairie region hunted in forests, not grasslands. The grasslands had been bullied south into the southern United States by the frigid advance of the glacier. When the Laurentide Ice Sheet was at its maximum extent, straddling the international border of the plains, a spruce forest extended from the ice margin, south into Kansas. As the glacier slowly retreated, the forest followed. Tree stumps and other remains of these past postglacial forests are occasionally unearthed when ditches are dug. Close on the heels of the retreating forest were the grasslands. By 8000 years ago the glacier had withdrawn far enough north to restore warmer and drier conditions to the Canadian prairie region, and the grasslands returned.

Climate

Climate has always been the principal determinant in the distribution of vegetation, and it was the climate that orchestrated the postglacial return of the grasslands to the Canadian prairies. The climate of the mixed grass prairie is a cool, semi-arid one, characterized by extremes. In winter temperatures may plummet to $-50°C$, forcing rocks to wince, and in summer temperatures can climb to an intolerable $+40°C$. These seasonal extremes occur because of the interior location of the prairies. Oceans, with their voluminous heat-holding capacity, moderate the climate of coastal regions, but the centres of continents enjoy no such amelioration. In Swift Current, Saskatchewan, in the heart of the mixed grass prairie, the average maximum January temperature is $-18°C$. At the same latitude on the coast of British Columbia the average daily maximum is $+2°C$.

Extremes in temperature are also a daily pattern. The humidity of the prairies is low, and with little water vapour or clouds to block the heating rays of the sun, daytime temperatures can easily climb. At night, again with the low humidity, there is too little moisture in the air to stall the cooling of the earth, and air temperatures drop. The low humidity, however, provides the prairies with more hours of sunshine than any other region in Canada.

Lying in the rain shadow of the Rocky Mountains, the mixed grass prairie receives little precipitation. The annual precipitation averages between 30-40 centimeters, with half of the moisture falling between April and July and a quarter of it falling as snow. But an average is just that, and yearly precipitation levels can swing between 10 centimeters and 60 centimeters. The driest regions of the mixed grass prairie are the adjacent corners of southern Alberta and southern Saskatchewan. From this point the precipitation increases to the north, the west and the east. During the lean years the specter of drought returns, and with it, memories of the 1930's. Between 1930 and 1939 there was progressively less rain each year until 1937. The dust blew and crops failed. Farmers squinted into the sun for a hint of respite. But the temperament of the prairies is written in stone, and the hopes and dreams of men have never changed a word.

Winds add another dimension to the character of the prairies. Cowboys advise not to exert yourself if you lose your hat to a prairie wind, but to sit for a while, and grab the next one that rolls by. The mixed grass prairie is flushed by winds from the west that blow strongest between March and May. The winds are often dry and tug at the moisture in plants and soil. Though the prairies receive 30-40 centimeters of moisture annually, the evaporation rate may exceed that three times over, making the area more arid than expected. Warm dessicating winds from the southwest, called *chinooks*, are the harshest on plants. These winds are strongest near the mountains, and gradually wane as they move east. But the chinooks bring a welcome reprieve from the icy grip of winter. In a matter of hours they can raise the temperature from subzero levels to above freezing.

Microclimate

On a typical day in May when the weatherman reports clear skies and a temperature of 25°C, a person knows what to expect. But on the same day the conditions will be dramatically different on the clay slopes of the badlands, the grassy tops of buttes or beneath the congested shrubbery of coulees. In each of these areas, soil moisture, humidity, wind velocity, sunlight and temperature varies, and they combine to create a whole spectrum of "mini" climates, or microclimates. It is the microclimate that concerns wildlife, and it determines the fine features of plant distribution. Let us consider a number of aspects of microclimate in detail. North facing slopes, for example, are consistently cooler and suffer less evaporation than slopes that face south, and slopes in general retain less moisture and experience higher rates of runoff than level areas. Because of wind, elevated areas are cooler than depressions in summer, and suffer less frost damage in spring and autumn. Vegetation, as well as the topography, has an effect on the microclimate. The foliage of plants protects the ground against extremes of temperature, reduces the velocity of the wind (and thus the drying effects) and adds moisture to the air through the respiration of its leaves.

Because of all of these factors, animals, especially small ones, have a variety of microclimates from which to choose, and they frequently vary their selection with the seasons. We find a similar responsiveness to microclimate in plants. Any given hill in the mixed grass prairie may be vegetated by a different set of plants on each of its four sides — the plants capitalizing on the subtle differences in soil, sunlight, temperature and moisture.

The five different habitats of the mixed grass prairie result primarily from five slightly different microclimates. The different microclimates have determined the characteristic vegetation and wildlife present in each habitat. The next chapter deals with the most extensive of the five prairie habitats, the flat to gently rolling grassland plains.

Caves moderate the climate, and the natural caverns of the badlands have been used by Indians, outlaws, mammals, birds, spiders and snakes.

The mixed grasslands is one of the most arid regions of Canada, receiving 30-40 centimeters of rain a year.

The seeds of common speargrass are barbed, and they have a long tail that twists in response to changes in the humidity, literally screwing the seed into the ground.

Bulrushes are emergent plants that commonly occupy the deep water offshore from cattails. Pictured is the great bulrush, one of three grassland species, which features a round, spongy stem that can grow to a height of 2.5 meters.

Once winter has released its grip, ice sculptures skirt the edge of prairie streams.

Clay swells when it absorbs water. When it dries, the surface dries first, contracting and forming cracks.

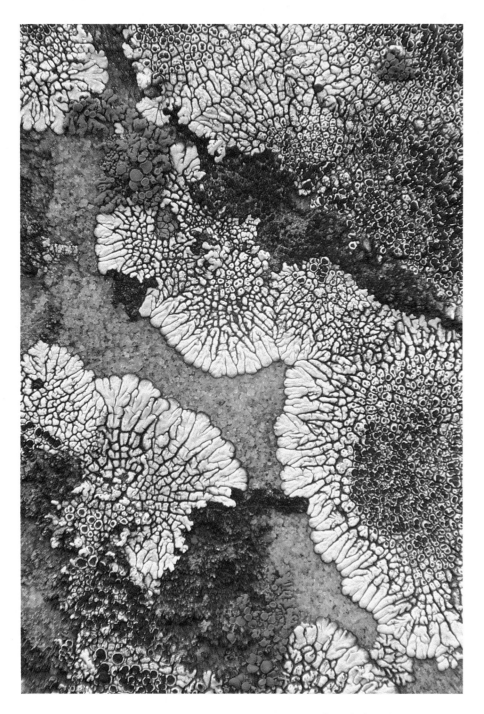

Lichens were the earliest plants to recolonize the denuded landscape in the wake of the retreating glacier.

All sedimentary rock, like this sandstone, is deposited in layers.

The resistant, ironstone caprock of these hoodoos protects the underlying soft sandstone from erosion.

To compete for light, wildflowers, such as the golden bean, must grow taller than the neighbouring grasses.

The pronghorn is the fastest animal in North America; speeds of 80 kph have been recorded.

The trembling aspen is a graceful tree whose root system is shallow, wide-spreading and generally produces underground stems. Reproduction by underground stems is the main method of propagation of this species, and extensive forests composed entirely of aspen have developed in this way.

Hoarfrost encases the fruits of a wild rose.

A hoodoo in the Milk River region.

The bentonite clay surface of the badlands.

Crested wheatgrass was introduced into North America from Russia because of its drought resistance.

The Level Plains

Of the five habitats of the mixed grass prairie, the gently rolling plains is the one which is most familiar. It is a soft and easy landscape, flat, or gently ruffled into waves of rolling hills. Here, the sun and clouds finger the land with light and shadow, and change its character by the minute. And everywhere there is grass, with a peaceful grip on the land.

The Grass Plant

Grasses evolved some 60 million years ago from tropical woody ancestors, of which the bamboo is a present day example. The tenacity and resilience of grasses have enabled them to tackle frigid tundra, searing sand dunes, rarefied alpine slopes, marshes, swamps and deserts. But grasses reach their greatest luxuriance and diversity in the grasslands of the world. Worldwide there are over 4000 species of grasses, with 100 or so of these growing in the mixed grass prairie of Canada. Grasses are commonly divided into shortgrasses (less than 0.5 meters), midgrasses (0.5-1.5 meters) and tallgrasses (1.5-3.0 meters). The mixed grass prairie is composed of both shortgrasses and midgrasses, the predominance of each dependent upon the precipitation. In the moister peripheral regions of the mixed grass prairie, midgrasses dominate, and in years of above average precipitation, they may flourish throughout the entire region. In normal years the shortgrasses (such as blue grama) grow in the driest sections of the region, but they become more widespread in years of drought.

Grass can be trampled, buried, broken or burnt, and still it comes back. Natural selection has honed it to endure. Grasses have an extensively branched root system that absorbs moisture from the most niggardly shower — an adaptation which is obviously beneficial in the semi-arid climate of the mixed grass prairie. In an often cited experiment conducted in the 1930's, a single rye grass plant produced 620 kilometers of roots in just four months. When the plant's 15 billion root hairs (the fine structures through which water and minerals are absorbed) were included, the total length was greater than the distance from Vancouver to Halifax and back again, and the surface area equalled that of two basketball courts.

The astonishing root density of grass plants holds the soil in place and protects the land against erosion. Such root density also enabled the prairie settlers of the late 1800's to cut the soil into building blocks and construct homes of sod. The sod houses provided good protection against the cold, the heat and the wind, but rain was another matter. It was said that if it rained outside for a day it would rain inside for two.

Grasses have hollow stems strengthened by solid nodes, or knobs, that enable the plant to bend in the wind without breaking. Even if a grass plant is trampled down, the tissue on the lower side of the nodes can elongate and straighten the plant back up towards the light.

Because of their thrifty management of water, grasses do well in regions of low precipitation. The leaves of grasses have a thick surface layer that resists evaporation, and their pores, through which carbon dioxide and oxygen are exchanged, are recessed in grooves along the leaf surface, which buffers them from the drying effects of air currents. Some grasses have additional protection against dessication. The leaves of grasses such as the northern and western wheatgrass have large, thin-walled cells on the leaf surface. These lose water more readily than usual surface cells so that when the grass is water stressed, the loss of turgor in these large cells causes the leaves to roll into a tight tube. This effectively reduces the surface area of the leaf that is exposed to the drying effects of the wind. Without this mechanism the grass plant would just wilt.

A grass blade grows from its base rather than its tip; thus it can be cropped by grazing animals and still continue to grow. Also, the critical growing parts of the grass plant are located at or below the ground surface, and this protects the grass from fire. This last structural characteristic has certainly been instrumental in maintaining and possibly expanding the mixed grass prairie region in Canada over the last 10,000 years. The Plains Indians routinely ignited the prairies in warfare and hunting. These recurrent fires were devastating to shrubs and trees attempting to secure a foothold in the grasslands region, and this perpetuated the dominance of the more fire resistant grasses. Grasses rebounded quickly after every fire.

Prairie Wildflowers

Though different species of grasses comprise greater than 80% of the vegetation of this land, hundreds of varieties of wildflowers colour the prairie landscape. The prairie crocus is the first wildflower to bloom, usually about the middle of April. Some Plains Indians believed that the crocus was more than a portent of spring, it was an opportunity for reflection. When a man found his first flower of the year he would light his pipe and sit nearby. After ceremoniously anointing the earth, the sky and the four compass points he would contemplate his past and future life. After a period of peaceful introspection he would reverently empty the ashes near the flower and continue on his journey, heartened by the experience.

The early wildflowers benefit from the moisture left by the melted snow, but they must also contend with unpredictable and, frequently, cool temperatures. As a consequence, moss phlox and early cinquefoil are short, and they hug the ground and grow in clusters, creating their own microclimate. Somewhat sheltered from the chilling winds of spring, temperatures within the clusters of flowers may be 5°C higher than the air above. The prairie crocus uses a different strategy to warm itself. Crocus flowers turn to face the sun throughout the day, and the disc shape of their blooms, like miniature disc antennae, focuses heat onto the centres of the flowers. After a cool night in April, the fuzzy stamens of the crocus flower are frequently crowded with beetles, flies, bees and spiders. The insects are attracted by the warmer microhabitat (sometimes greater than 10°C

warmer), and in the process the insects benefit the flower by inadvertently pollinating it.

As the months progress the varieties of blooming flowers become taller and taller to compete with the growing grasses for light. By late summer only the tallest flowers, such as, asters, goldenrods and sunflowers, are still in bloom.

Flowers Talk To Insects

For centuries flowers have inspired painters and poets, and their petals have frequently helped me to determine whether I was loved or not, but these are not their reasons for being. Flowers talk to insects.

Flowers contain both female and male parts in the centre of their blossoms. Although some flowers can pollinate, or fertilize, themselves, in most instances a pollen grain (the male cell) from one plant unites with the ovule (the female cell) from another plant. This union produces a seed. Flowers face a problem in achieving this union since the plants are anchored by their roots to separate spots. The solution is a ménage à trois, with the wind or insects being the third party. (In other ecosystems birds and bats may also participate as pollinators.) To attract the different insects, flowers have evolved specialized structures, colours, odours and nectar glands. Generally, each flower tries to attract only one or two specific pollinators, and therefore prairie flowers can be grouped into bee flowers, moth flowers, fly flowers and wind flowers.

Flowers that attract bees are brightly coloured in blues and yellows, and they have a sweet odour. The petals of these flowers are arranged to provide a convenient landing platform, and the nectar glands at the base of the petals reward the bee. Since bees are diurnal, many of these flowers close at night. Among others, the prairie larkspurs and mints are good examples of bee flowers.

Moth flowers are invariably white and heavily scented to attract their nocturnal pollinators. Moths use their long tongues to reach the nectar glands and do not settle during feeding, so the flowers they pollinate do not need landing platforms. The wild morning glory is a moth flower.

Flies are not attracted by sight but by odours, and many flies are attracted by the odours of dung, humus, and carrion. The prairie carrionflower is a small, dull greenish-white blossom that has evolved to attract flies, deceiving them with its carrion-like odour.

Finally there is the large group of flowers that rely on the wind for pollination. Wind pollination was the first pollination strategy to evolve millions of years ago; today it still plays a very important part in grassland plants. Wind-pollinated flowers have no need for bright colours, nectar glands, sweet odours or landing platforms. Most do not even have petals, which would only act as barriers to windborne pollen. Grasses are married to the wind, for they all have wind-pollinated flowers. But the flowers are so dull and inconspicuous that it surprises many people to learn that grasses have flowers at all.

Wildlife frequently ignores categories that scientists contrive, and insect pollinators are no exception. Any given flower may be visited by beetles, butterflies, bees and flies, and any one of these may accidentally pollinate the flower. This does not invalidate what has been said about the various pollination strategies of flowers, it merely illustrates that the system is a flexible one.

The Dispersal of Seeds

Prairie grasses and wildflowers require the wind, birds, animals and insects for another function: to disperse their seeds. In autumn, the wind plucks countless Russian thistles, or tumbleweeds, from their moorings and sends them wandering across the level plains. They cluster for a while in hollows and stack against fences, but when the wind changes direction they are whipped into motion again. Each tumbleweed carries tens of thousands of seeds that are released as it bounces along. The Russian thistle was introduced into the northern plains of the United States in the late 1800's, and within a few scant decades it had established itself throughout the entire grasslands of North America, a convincing testimonial to the efficiency of the wind as a dispersal agent.

Grass seeds may stick to the muddy feet of wading birds

and be transported from one waterhole to another. Even seeds that are ingested may survive. Viable seeds have been recovered from bird droppings more than five days after they were eaten, and in five days a bird in migration can fly thousands of kilometers, contributing to a wide distribution of seeds. Passing animals also disperse seeds. The seeds of porcupine grass and needle grass are barbed and catch easily on fur. Other animals, such as, ground squirrels and mice, gather and cache seeds which may later be forgotten by the animals, and eventually the seeds germinate.

The Humble Life of the Prairies

Some insects are also dispersal agents and none is more conspicuous than the industrious ant. Ants are social insects; they cannot survive alone, and they can belong only to the colony in which they developed. There are three castes in ant society: males, females and workers. In summer when conditions are right within the colony, winged male and female ants are produced. Then, in response to environmental cues such as specific temperatures or a rainfall, the winged ants fly from the nest. Ants from all of the colonies in an area usually emerge at the same time and swarm together. In this way mating occurs, and ants establish new colonies. The male dies shortly after the courtship flight, but the impregnated female digs a small sheltered chamber in the soil and lays her eggs. The female, called the queen, sheds her wings, and the large muscles that she used for her nuptial flight are resorbed to provide nutrients to sustain her until her first brood of eggs hatches. The new hatchlings develope into workers which will then feed her.

Ants intrigue people because they seem to display human qualities, such as, sociability, industriousness and allegiance. In the mixed grass prairie there are several dozen species of ants, and, like people, the ants make their living in a variety of ways. They hunt, harvest, herd, enslave and conquer.

Hunting ants are the most common ants in the prairies. They immobilize their insect prey by curving their abdomens forward underneath and spraying formic acid between their legs. Harvester ants build conspicuous mounds, and they can be distinguished from all other prairie ants by their long waist. Harvester ants collect seeds which they first coat with saliva that has antibiotic properties, and then store in underground granaries, sometimes five meters below the surface. Harvester ants fastidiously clip the vegetation from around their mounds, and it is speculated that this prevents root channels from developing into the underlying granaries, which would allow water to seep in and spoil the grain.

The red and black thatching ant builds large mounds, like harvester ants, but it covers the domes with twigs and broken grass stems. Colonies of thatching ants may contain 40,000 individuals. The thatching ant is sometimes a hunter and often a herder. These ants herd groups of aphids, frequently called "ant cows." Aphids are tiny insects that suck the juices out of plants. They then produce a kind of nectar which the ants in turn ingest. The thatching ants are very attentive to the aphids and protect them from predators.

Other prairie ants display characteristics reminiscent of the darker side of man. Slave-making ants steal eggs from other colonies and when the eggs hatch the ants are used as workers. In the mixed grass prairie large red ants are often found in the mounds of the common black field ant. The red ant is a conqueror. A conquering red queen invades another colony and disposes of the existing queen. She then lays her own eggs which are cared for by the resident workers. Eventually the conquerors outnumber their subjects.

Ants are silent insects, but the grasshoppers of the prairies explode from underfoot in noisy, buzzing flight. The clear-winged and red-legged grasshoppers are common on the mixed grass prairie, and in some years there are heavy infestations of them. Grasshoppers lay their eggs in late summer and early autumn. The female repeatedly thrusts the tip of her abdomen into the soil and lays up to 1500 eggs in 10-20 separate pods. The eggs overwinter in the ground and hatch in the spring as miniature adults without wings. Through the summer, with 5-6 moults, the grasshoppers grow to adult size, and they become winged with the final moult. When there is a warm autumn the egg-laying period is extended and more eggs can be laid. When this is followed by a cool spring, and then a dry summer, the grasshopper population swells to its maximum. Cool spring weather delays hatching so that when the young emerge, plants have started to grow and there is a good supply of food. Dry summers prevent the growth of fungus which normally infects grasshoppers and keeps their numbers in check.

Grasshoppers are near the start of the food chain, so when they are plentiful, other prairie wildlife benefits. Dead grasshoppers are consumed by ants, beetles and crickets. Their eggs are eaten by skunks and curlews, and the adults and young are prey for meadowlarks, magpies, burrowing owls and many other birds.

Birds of the Level Plains

Birds are the most conspicuous residents of the mixed grass prairie, and of the several hundred species recorded, over a hundred of them breed within the region, and many of them are unique.

The flat, treeless plains are a habitat that presents a special challenge to grassland birds. The plains offer birds few elevated perches from which to sing, provide little foliage in which to hide their nests, and assure good visibility for their predators. To survive, the birds of the grasslands have evolved fascinating adaptations to deal with each of these challenges.

Male birds sing to inform other males of their presence in a territory and to attract females. In the forested regions of Canada, birds commonly sing from exposed treetops and elevated branches where they can project their calls and be seen. Grassland birds, such as pipits, longspurs and lark buntings, make themselves noticeable by singing on the wing, during choreographed aerial flights over their territories. The black and white lark bunting rises several meters into the air, fixes its wings rigidly above the level of its back, and then gradually floats down in a circle, or an arc, pouring out a series of buzzes and trills. Another noted aerial songster is the high-flying Sprague's pipit. This pipit hangs in the sky, almost out of sight, sometimes for an hour or so, circling and delivering its thin metallic jingle.

The absence of trees also affects the nesting behavior of grassland birds, and most of the birds of the level plains habitat build their nests on the ground. The nests of curlews, killdeers, sparrows, larks and others are either simple hollow depressions in the ground with little added material, or small grassy cups, lined with fine feathers and hair, hidden in the grass. All of these birds have heavily patterned backs of greys and browns to blend with their surroundings, and the eggs of many of them are blotched and streaked, which protects the eggs when the parents are away from the nest.

Most interesting of all, though, is the acting ability of grassland birds. Many of them have a series of displays meant to distract and lure away predators that approach dangerously close to the nest. Usually the bird flaps laboriously about the ground, dragging its tail and wings. Soon the predator is in hot pursuit of a seemingly easy victim, but the bird eludes capture by flying off. The fooled animal then moves away in a new direction, usually missing the nest.

The Lives of Nestlings

Nestlings are classified into two groups, either altricial or precocial. Familiar to most are altricial nestlings that are born blind, naked, and helpless, and totally dependent on their parents. The nestlings of most of the grassland songbirds are altricial, but all of the grouse and shorebirds that nest on the plains have precocial nestlings. These precocial birds start life as down-covered chicks that are able to leave the nest soon after they hatch. This precociousness confers a certain survival advantage. Chicks that move out of the nest and disperse, rather than staying huddled together, are less likely to fall prey to a fox or coyote. In the precocial group of nestlings there are varying degrees of dependence. Sharp-tailed grouse and sage grouse show their young which foods to eat, but the chicks of other birds find their own food, although they continue to follow their parents. All precocial young rely on their parents to sound an alarm when danger threatens. When

the alarm is sounded the chicks stay motionless until it is safe, their protective cryptic colouration helping to conceal them from predators.

The Dancer, The Gypsy, and The Trickster

The behavior of wildlife, particularly that of birds, is the aspect of their lives that fascinates me most. The strategies of courtship and nest selection are intriguing and a challenge to interpret. The sage grouse, cowbird and burrowing owl are three of my favorites, and their behavior deserves a closer look.

The sage grouse is the largest grouse in North America, and in Canada it is found only in the mixed grass prairie. The principal reason for this is sagebrush, which grows only in the drier regions of the mixed grasslands and is the staple winter food of the sage grouse.

Every spring the sage grouse gather at traditional dancing grounds to court and mate. At dawn and dusk, throughout April and into May, the male grouse display together. Each bird struts and puffs on its own small territory, which it defends against all other males. The territories in the centre of the dancing grounds are held by the dominant birds which have had to compete with other males to win these favoured positions. Females, alone or in groups, wander through the collection of males, and 90% of the hens mate with the 10% of male grouse that occupy the favoured locations in the centre of the dancing grounds. Thus, the mating strategy of the sage grouse ensures that the hens mate with dominant males, the healthiest and most vigourous birds, which in turn ensures that offspring receive the best genetic endowment.

The cowbird earned its name from its habit of associating with cattle. The birds perch on the backs of cows and horses and pick off lice and ticks, or else they follow on the ground and capture insects disturbed by the grazing animals. Years ago, cowbirds were called buffalo birds, and they followed the migrating herds of bison. But this presented a problem. How could the birds keep pace with the movements of the great herds and also attend to hungry youngsters back at the nest? The solution for the buffalo bird was to lay its eggs in other birds' nests, allowing foster parents to raise the young and freeing itself to follow the bison. The foster parents were usually smaller birds such as sparrows or warblers, so that the alien egg, usually one per nest, "hatched a monster." The buffalo bird nestling, being larger, took most of the food and grew the fastest, in the same way that cowbird nestlings do today, thus guaranteeing the survival of the species.

The cowbird was successful in its transition from bison to cattle, but the future of the burrowing owl is less assured. The burrowing owl is a small (25 centimeters tall), long-legged, ground-dwelling owl of the mixed grass prairie. The owl uses the abandoned burrows of badgers and ground squirrels for its nest. Early in the nesting season the adults collect dried manure and pile it on the mound at the entrance of their burrow. When the pile is big enough the owls shred the manure and spread some of it around the entrance of the burrow. The remainder of the manure is used to line their nest cavity and the 2-3 meter tunnel that leads to it. If you remove the manure, as I once did in a moment of mischievousness, the owls replace it within 24 hours. Biologists speculate that the manure masks the owl's scent from predatory badgers, or perhaps alerts ground squirrels and prairie dogs so that they do not inadvertently enter the burrow.

Burrows are important to the owls, not only as nesting sites, but as refuges from danger. When a golden eagle or coyote is sighted, the owls often plunge underground rather than flying off. The burrowing owl defends its burrow in an unusual way. To discourage intruders adult and young owls can mimic the buzzing of a rattlesnake. Since rattlesnakes also use abandoned burrows, the owl's sham is a clever one.

Today, throughout the mixed grass prairie, the existence of the burrowing owl is threatened. Several explanations have been proposed for this decline: secondary poisoning of the owl; the conversion of native pastures to agricultural land resulting in temporary loss of burrows; and the destruction of burrowing mammals that normally supply the owls with burrows. In Canada, fewer than 2000 pairs of burrowing owls

are left. Strict protection and careful management are essential if the burrowing owl is to remain in our mixed grass prairie.

Life Down Under

The burrow dwellers of the grasslands are many. These include the burrowing owl, the black-tailed prairie dog, the Richardson ground squirrel, the badger, the Nuttall's cottontail rabbit and the prairie rattlesnake. Burrows provide these animals with a less severe microclimate and shelter them from the extremes of weather. Seasonal temperature swings are less drastic in burrows. In summer they are cooler than the open plains and in winter they are warmer. The humidity within burrows is higher than aboveground, so that less body moisture is lost to the environment.

Richardson ground squirrels live in loose, rambling colonies of several dozen animals. The ground squirrels follow an unusual life pattern in which adult males are active for only three months and hibernate for the rest of the year. Each year the adult male ground squirrels are the first to emerge from hibernation in early March. The females come out of hibernation several weeks later. After a brief mating encounter the male is banished from the female's territory. The scarred rumps of many male ground squirrels bear testimony of the strength of the female's convictions. The newborn ground squirrels appear at the end of May, and by then many adult males have already re-entered hibernation. Most adult females will hibernate by early July, and from then until September only the young are active. The early hibernation of adult ground squirrels appears premature. It seems more reasonable that the animals would need as much time as possible to feed and accumulate fat stores before tackling hibernation with its inherent risks, but this pattern may be important in preventing competition between adults and young for food resources. Moreover, adult males have no important function once mating is completed, and although the females stay until the young are self-sufficient, they also have a limit to their biological usefulness.

The black-tailed prairie dog, a close relative of the

Richardson ground squirrel, does not hibernate and is a much more gregarious animal, living in large colonies called "dogtowns." Whereas the Richardson ground squirrel is found throughout the mixed grasslands, the prairie dog is restricted to a small area of the mixed grass prairie along the Frenchman River in southwestern Saskatchewan. The dogtowns here contain several hundred animals, but in Texas in the 1800's there was a prairie dog megalopolis that measured 160 kilometers by 400 kilometers and contained 400 million prairie dogs.

Dogtowns attract a host of other prairie wildlife. Ants, beetles and spiders come for the manure and each other; horned larks, meadowlarks and longspurs come for the insects; and prairie falcons come for the longspurs and larks. The plump prairie dogs attract the larger predators of the grasslands, and if you watch a dogtown long enough you will see coyotes, badgers and golden eagles.

The black-tailed prairie dog and the Richardson ground squirrel share similar adaptations to an underground lifestyle in a flat, treeless habitat. Both squirrels have high-set eyes which facilitate the detection of aerial predators, and both squirrels produce alarm calls that alert others in the colony when predators are near. They both have short front legs and long claws for digging, and both have small ears which keep dirt from accumulating.

On Rattlesnakes

The rattlesnake's range just edges into the mixed grass prairie region of Canada, in a 50-kilometer-wide band along the international border, with a smaller isolated population along the South Saskatchewan River. No grassland snake has been more maligned or persecuted than the rattlesnake, yet it is a marvel — none is more suitably adapted to its environment.

The rattlesnake is unique among snakes of the grasslands because it has heat detectors on its face, obviating the need for the snake to see when it hunts. Just as we can sense the direction of a fireplace from the heat that it throws on our face, rattlesnakes locate mice and ground squirrels, in complete darkness, by detecting the heat these warm-blooded animals emit. Its heat detectors are located in a pair of pits between the eye and nostril. A thin membrane, one-quarter the thickness of this page, stretches across the back of each pit and is crammed with nerve endings that pick up infrared radiation. The rattlesnake's heat-detecting capacity is extremely sensitive, and the snake can detect temperature differences as subtle as 3/1000 of a degree.

The poison glands of the rattlesnake, which give the snake's head its triangular shape, are modified salivary glands; these glands probably started out as aids to digestion and only later acquired their defensive function. The composition of venom is complex — over three dozen separate chemicals have already been identified. The fangs, which inject the venom, are hinged in the front of the jaw and fold along the roof of the snake's mouth. When the rattlesnake strikes, it throws its head back and the fangs spring down and project straight forward.

Every Plains Indian tribe had its own remedy for rattlesnake bites. Typically, special plants were eaten raw, boiled, or as a broth, or else applied as a poultice. Usually these measures were combined with the incantations and ministrations of the medicine man. Early cowboys used a hot branding iron to neutralize the poison, or they would pour gun powder over the wound and ignite it. This method had questionable therapeutic effect, but it certainly distracted the attention of the victim.

Others used poultices of frogs, toads and mice. The more repulsive the therapy the greater its merit. In the end, however, the chicken won. Practitioners of the poultry school of snakebite therapy suggested that a whole chicken be split and applied as a poultice, being certain that the head and feathers of the chicken were retained. When the flesh of the chicken turned green, or the comb turned blue, the therapy was complete — a foul cure.

The Sagebrush Speedster

Pronghorn spend the greater part of their lives in loose herds, and they are endowed with great speed, endurance and acute vision. These are desirable traits for an animal that inhabits a flat, open environment. The pronghorn has also evolved a number of characteristics associated with its birth process that are crucial for its survival.

The birth process in the pronghorn is relatively long, extending over 2-3 hours. During labour, doe pronghorn look about, get up, and walk around in the immediate area. The ebb and flow of labour allows the pronghorn mother to be periodically alert to her surroundings and, if necessary, change birth sites. An animal that remained oblivious to its environment over a shorter period, for instance, 30 minutes, could likely be stalked by a predator more successfully.

Pronghorn mothers leave the birth site and their hidden offspring, usually twins, within three hours of delivery. It is important, therefore, for the mother to quickly establish a firm bond with her young. Does usually rise and begin to lick the newborn immediately upon birth. It is speculated that this instinctual grooming, possibly triggered by the smell of the birth fluids, is essential for maternal imprinting and individual recognition of her young, and imparts in the mother the necessary attentiveness that will assure the survival of her offspring.

Man on the Plains

The Plains Indians were nomadic hunters and gatherers. Like all cultures based on a similar economy the Plains Indians had few possessions, and they left relatively few artifacts. However, they did leave behind structures of stones that give us some insight into their lives. Scattered throughout the mixed grass prairie are tipi rings, medicine wheels and boulder effigies.

Tipi rings were made when Indians placed rocks around the base of their conical tents to anchor them against the perpetual prairie winds. When the people moved their camps, the rocks were left behind as circles of stones 4-5 meters in diameter. Although I have found tipi rings on the level plains and in coulees and river bottoms, they are often found on the edge of escarpments where the former inhabitants could watch for game and enemy tribes.

Medicine wheels were named because of their appearance. At least 50 medicine wheels have been located in the mixed grass prairies east of the Rockies. The wheels follow a general pattern, and usually consist of a central cairn of rocks with 6-24 spokes radiating out from the centre. At times another circle of rocks encloses the spokes. The purpose of the wheels is more difficult to explain than their appearance. One popular theory proposes that the spokes of the wheels were designed to align with certain celestial bodies during the summer solstice, the longest day of the year. This was the season of the Sun Dance, celebrated by all prairie tribes, and medicine wheels may have functioned as calendars. Others believe that the wheels were monuments commemorating propitious events, or the exploits of a hero. One particular medicine wheel in Alberta is believed to be a memorial to Many Spotted Horses, a Blood war chief. The spokes of the wheel represent his many battle victories.

Boulder effigies were made by placing stones on the ground to outline a figure. Favorite themes were turtles, buffalo, and men. The effigies were built on bare hilltops and sometimes occurred in association with tipi rings. The figures depicted may represent legendary spirits. The turtle was part of the mythology of the Sioux and Assiniboine tribes, and there is a well-known legend involving a turtle. In this legend the hero is helped by a turtle and the animal is rewarded with a thick shell to protect it from biting insects in its lakeside home.

The Indians moved with the seasons and the bison, and in winter they abandoned the exposed level plains habitat, with its harsh, bitter cold, for sheltered areas such as the Great Sand Hills region of western Saskatchewan. There are sandhill areas in all three prairie provinces, and this habitat will be considered next.

The highly adaptable coyote was originally restricted to the grasslands, but it has expanded its range over the last century to cover most of North America, except for the Arctic.

The sage grouse is the largest grouse in North America; males weigh 2.5-3 kilograms.

The blooms of the gumbo evening primrose are white when they open, but they quickly fade to a delicate pink by the end of the same day.

The golden bean is poisonous to humans in both the flower and the seed stage.

The western red lily is the provincial flower of Saskatchewan.

The slender-leaved, blue-eyed grass is a wildflower that grows in clumps; it is easily mistaken for a grass when the plant is not in flower.

A young grasshopper shelters in a tuft of foxtail barley. Grasshoppers hatch as miniature adults without wings. After five or six months they reach maturity and acquire wings in the final moult.

The undulating topography of southwestern Saskatchewan is an aftermath of the Ice Age. When the relief is less than six meters it is called ground moraine, and when, as in this case, it varies between six and eighteen meters it is called knob and kettle topography.

The precocious young killdeer leaves its nest within hours of hatching. It relies on its cryptic coloration to camouflage it against predators.

The long-billed curlew is the largest bird in the Sandpiper Family; it is 45 centimeters long with a bill that adds an additional 21 centimeters. Incubation is shared by both sexes and the bird pictured is sitting on a clutch of four spotted eggs.

The prairie rattlesnake adds a new rattle to its tail each time it sheds its skin. Young rattlesnakes moult soon after they are born, and in the first year of life, when growth is most rapid, there may be 3 or 4 moults. In subsequent years the skin is usually shed soon after emergence from hibernation, but the frequency of moulting decreases as age increases and the growth rate slows.

Indian rice grass.

Alkali grass.

A pair of pronghorn bucks wrestle to establish dominance. Their horns lock them together so that the fight becomes a contest of strength with a minimum of injuries.

The eyes of the plains garter snake, as with most snakes, differ from other vertebrates in that they lack a fovea — the area of the retina designed to give greater definition. Although their vision is blurred, snakes readily perceive movement, and their laterally directed eyes give them a very wide field of view.

The alarm call of the Richardson ground squirrel alerts other animals in the colony to potential danger, and the animal's highset eyes are well adapted to the detection of aerial predators.

Owls swallow their prey whole, or in large pieces, and regurgitate the indigestibles in neat compact pellets containing hair, teeth, bone and the exoskeletons of insects. The analysis of pellets makes it easy to study the food habits of owls. The diminuitive burrowing owl, pictured here, eats crickets, grasshoppers, mice and small snakes.

Windscapes

As I strolled back to my camp in the Great Sand Hills of Saskatchewan a porcupine shuffled across the dunes. I was upwind from the animal, and it stopped when it caught my scent. I moved slowly to one side and it ambled on, the quills of its tail inscribing its signature in the sand. It was the end of the day and the sunset held additional promise. The sun stalked the dunes with a fiery eye, and anything that blocked its view was burdened with a lengthy shadow. As the eye reclined the fire spread and streaked the clouds with crimson. The ebb and flow of colour imbued the sky with life, and the clumps of clouds shrank and swelled like the heaving of great lungs. And then it was over, and the molten sky cooled, and the porcupine was somewhere in the night.

The sandhill areas are the least extensive of the five habitats of the mixed grass prairie, and some would argue that they are so widely scattered and of such small extent that they do not merit separate consideration. But the unique character of sandhill areas, in particular the Great Sand Hills of Saskatchewan, with their unusual blend of wildlife and plants, warrants a separate chapter.

The mixed grassland region of each of the prairie provinces has its sandhill areas. In Alberta there are isolated clusters of long, narrow, grass-covered dunes near Brooks Taber and Lethbridge, and north of Medicine Hat the Middle Sand Hills straddle the South Saskatchewan River. In Manitoba there are the Lauder Sandhills southwest of Brandon, and the Carberry Sandhills located in Spruce Woods Provincial Park. In Saskatchewan there are the Great Sand Hills — 1900 square kilometers of sand flats and dunes located north of the Trans Canada Highway near the Alberta border. The Great Sand Hills represent the best of the sandhills habitats, and the following sections describe this area. Naturally, much of what will be covered applies to all of the sandhill habitats.

The Shapes of the Wind

The Laurentide Ice Sheet started its final withdrawal from the southern prairies 15,000-18,000 years ago, ending the Wisconsin Glaciation which had lasted 100,000 years, and marking the start of the present interglacial period. In the immediate postglacial period the prairies were barren and devoid of vegetation, and the wind had a free hand to work the land. Sands from the beaches of old glacial lakes and from outwash plains were attacked by the wind and shaped into dunes. With time, vegetation returned and stabilized the sand, robbing the wind of its monopoly. Today the Great Sand Hills consist of an agglomeration of three identifiable landforms: stabilized dunes covered with grasses and shrubs; active dunes of barren sand; and sand flats, both vegetated and barren.

Dunes are always moving but their level of activity is not constant. Dune movement is greatest during periods of aridity, when drought denudes the sand of vegetation and makes it more vulnerable to the wind. The dunes of the Great Sand Hills have moved 1.5-4 kilometers since wind erosion started 10,000 years ago, but most of the dune movement occurred prior to 4000 years ago when there were greater periods of drought.

The three different landforms of the Great Sand Hills: the sand flats, active dunes, and stabilized dunes, produce different microclimates which in turn host different plant communities.

Sand flats are either high or low. The sand flats which occupy low-lying regions are generally the most fertile for two reasons: they trap fine, windblown silt and clay particles which enhance the soil by their greater capacity to hold water; and water is in greater supply because of runoff from adjacent dunes. This is where you will find water-loving willows, aspens and river birches, with an understory of juniper and rose shrubs. The soil in some low areas accumulates salts, and where this occurs a saline grassland develops with salt-tolerant species like arrowgrass, alkali grass and salt grass being the predominant plants. Salty soils will be considered again in Chapter 6.

The active dune landscape is the landscape that comes to mind when most of us think of sandhills. Here, the wind labours over the dunes, brushing the slopes with waves of ripples and drawing the crests into comforting curves. Today active dunes cover less than 1% of the Great Sand Hills. It is a landscape that is shifting and moving under the influence of the predominantly westerly wind. The ripples that form on the surface of the dune, at right angles to the wind, represent the distance that a grain of sand hops ahead when it is lifted by the wind. Presently the dunes are advancing three meters a year.

The active dunes are a hostile environment for plants and animals. Surface temperatures frequently rise above 50°C. in summer. Even when it rains, the moisture quickly percolates through the porous sand beyond the reach of most shallow-rooted grasses and shrubs. Nonetheless, over the millenia, plants colonized, conquered and stabilized the dunes. The earliest grasses to pioneer the dunes are sand dropseed, Indian rice grass, and sand reed grass, all tenacious species with deep roots that reach to the water table. Once these pioneer grasses have secured a foothold and quieted the shifting sands, other grasses and shrubs can move in. But the stabilization of active dunes is a slow, tenuous process. Periods of drought can tip the balance in favour of the dunes, and vegetation will die, erasing the results of hundreds of years of growth.

The stabilized dunes are sand dunes that have been subdued by a succession of plants until ground cover is almost complete. This is the most extensive of the three sandhill landscapes, and comprises over one half of the area of the Great Sand Hills.

Several microclimates can exist on a single stabilized dune if the dune is sufficiently high. North facing slopes, which have more moisture and are cooler, support dense growths of snowberry, Wood's rose, silverberry, chokecherry and gooseberry. The drier, warmer, south-facing slopes usually support grasslands of June grass and speargrass, or scattered growths of silver sagebrush and creeping juniper.

The variety of environments found within the Great Sand Hills supports a wide array of wildlife in large numbers Found there is the largest population of sharp-tailed grouse in Canada, and one of the largest populations of mule deer in Saskatchewan. Here there are animals that are rarely seen elsewhere, like the Great Plains and spadefoot toads, and Ord's kangaroo rat. As well as these there are at least a hundred other vertebrates and many more beetles, bugs and spiders.

The Timing of Life

In the evolution of life those animals that bred when clement weather, food and shelter were available had a greater survival of offspring than those that bred at less propitious times. Thus, natural selection favoured those animals that could time their breeding cycles best. Animals use a number of environmental cues as timing devices: tidal cycles, rainfall cycles, temperatures and the seasonal changes in daylength. In the temperate to northern latitudes it is the seasonal change in daylength that is the most reliable and consistent cue. It is the increasing daylength in March that is perceived by the brain of the sharp-tailed grouse, urging them to dance when all else is quiet. Under this stimulus the brain of the grouse produces a hormone that stimulates the recrudescence of the bird's testes or ovaries.

In the Great Sand Hills late March is an empty time. The landscape is leached of colour, and the bite of winter lingers as deer and pronghorn move slowly, rationing their strength. Silence pervades, the insects are locked in hibernation, and the songbirds are still a month away. The ground is frozen and brittle underfoot, the plants firmly held in check. But, out on a grassy knoll life refuses to be restrained, and the sharp-tails dance. Each spring the sharp-

tailed grouse assemble on ancestral dancing grounds to re-
enact the courtship ritual. The males coo, cluck and strut.
With their heads down and their tails pointed to the sky, they
rapidly stomp their feet, and little clouds of dust erupt
around them. The birds vibrate across the ground like
woundup toys; they run feverishly for a moment, and then
suddenly stop. Intermittently the female grouse wander
through the cluster of males looking for a mate. The
daylength, or *photoperiod*, not only coordinates the breeding
cycle of the sharp-tailed grouse, but synchronizes many other
aspecs of animal behavior and governs the lives of many
grassland mammals, birds and insects.

The photoperiod synchronizes the arrival and departure of
migrating birds, and the establishment of avian territories. It
times the seasonal changes in coat colour of weasels and hares,
and stimulates the growth of thick winter fur in coyotes and
badgers. The photoperiod drives ground squirrels into
hibernation, and it arrests the development of insects in a
phase preparatory for winter and then stimulates their
emergence in spring.

The changes in photoperiod are also the primary
determinants of antler growth in deer. The increasing
photoperiod in spring stimulates the pituitary gland in the
brain of the mule deer, and the hormones produced initiate
antler growth in April and May. The growing antlers are
covered with "velvet," a fur-covered skin that carries nerves
and blood vessels to the growing antler. Somewhat later,
different hormones from the pituitary gland, also under the
influence of daylength, stimulate growth of the testes. As the
rut approaches in the fall, male sex hormones from the
enlarging testes block the action of pituitary antler-growth
hormones, the antlers stop growing and the velvet dries up.
At this time the deer thrash their antlers against vegetation,
and as the velvet is rubbed off the antlers become polished
and stained brown with resin. Finally, as the photoperiod
shortens in late autumn and early winter the pituitary gland is
no longer stimulated, and this leads to a reduction of
stimulation of the testes. The resulting decrease of male sex
hormones leads to decalcification and weakening of the
connection between the antler and the deer's skull, and the
antlers are shed. The return of longer days in the spring starts
the cycle again.

Prairie Toads

Toads are usually associated with moist conditions, yet
the Great Plains toad and the plains spadefoot toad, two of
Canada's rarest varieties of toads, are found in the semi-arid
environment of the Great Sand Hills. It seems paradoxical
because the greatest problem that toads and all amphibians
face is dehydration, but within the Great Sand Hills there are
several large permanent lakes and a number of smaller
temporary ones that allow them to survive.

Toads breathe through lungs and through their skin. In
winter, toads hibernate by burying themselves in mud, and at
this time cutaneous respiration becomes more important than
pulmonary respiration. To be an effective respiratory organ,
skin must be moist, permeable and have a rich blood supply,
but these characteristics make the animal more vulnerable to
dehydration because of water loss through evaporation. To
protect itself from dehydration, the plains spadefoot toad may
stay buried deep in the soil for an entire year if conditions are
not moist enough for it to emerge. To minimize the danger of
dehydration, toads are active only at night when humidity is
high and temperatures are cooler.

Toads are also active at night because it is safer. Lacking
teeth or claws, toads are defenseless, and rely on nocturnal
activity, secretive behavior, cryptic coloration, and distasteful
skin secretions to protect them from predators. The skin of
most toads contains poison glands, but the poison is not
usually injurious to human skin. If a toad is eaten by a
predator, the toad's skin toxins cause nausea, respiratory and
muscle paralysis, and in some cases, death. The severity of the
reaction is proportionate to the size of the predator. For the
toad, this may seem like a very poor protective mechanism,
since it dies when it is eaten, but the strategy is aimed at the
welfare of the species rather than that of the individual. For
example, if a coyote eats a toad and gets sick, any toads

encountered thereafter will be left alone, and if the predator survives, chances are it will teach its offspring to avoid toads.

One grassland predator, the hognose snake, is a toad specialist. When a snake approaches a toad, the toad attempts to discourage the snake by inflating its body with air, thereby increasing its bulk by half. The hognose is rarely impressed by such tactics and once it captures the toad and starts to swallow it, a pair of specialized teeth on the rear of the snake's palate punctures and deflates the toad. The poisonous skin secretions of the toad do not affect the hognose snake which has large adrenal glands believed to detoxify the poison. The western hognose snake has not been found in the Great Sand Hills but ranges elsewhere throughout the mixed grass prairie.

Although toads are preyed upon by many animals, toads themselves are predators capturing insects and spiders with their long, sticky tongues. Of the numerous spiders known today, many of them were first described from partially digested specimens taken from the stomachs of toads. The spiders of the Great Sand Hills far outnumber the toads, and theirs is a different story.

Wolves With Eight Legs

Spiders are among the oldest terrestrial animals, dating back to the Carboniferous Period, 300 million years ago. Spiders are not insects. Insects have three body segments, three pairs of legs, and a pair of antennae; spiders have no antennae, only two body segments, and four pairs of legs. As well, spiders are distinctive in their feeding habits, their use of venom, and the many uses they have for silk.

Spiders have evolved into two broad categories, hunters and web-builders. The grasses of the prairie provide very poor anchorage for webs, so web-building spiders are relatively uncommon in the grasslands. Hunting spiders are very common, and among these, the wolf spiders are the most numerous in grassland regions. You can easily find the burrow of wolf spiders throughout the stabilized dunes of the Great Sand Hills. Like all hunting spiders, wolf spiders detect their prey by vision and rely very little on silk traps. They are active predators, and once they have sighted their prey, they pounce on it and subdue it with venom from their fangs. The prey of spiders is often as big or bigger than the spider's own body, and usually covered with a hard exoskeleton that is not easily torn apart. To solve this problem, spiders flood their prey with digestive juices from their mouth that transform the inside of the prey into a liquefied broth that is sucked up.

Most spiders have eight eyes, arranged in two rows of four each. The eyes of web-building spiders are small and relatively weak because they rely on vibrations transmitted through the silk strands of their web to alert them to the presence of prey. In contrast, wolf spiders have no web and they must sight their prey before they can catch it. These spiders also have eight eyes, but two of their eyes are greatly enlarged for greater visual acuity and far-sightedness.

Among all spiders, wolf spider mothers display an unmatched attentiveness to their eggs and young. The female attaches her silken egg sac to the tip of her abdomen and carries the sac at all times. When the young hatch, the mother spider bites the egg sac to release the young spiderlings, which pour out of the sac and immediately climb onto her back. Very often there is more than one layer of spiderlings, and to deal with this the mother's back is covered with special knobbed hairs that allow the spiderlings to hold on. The young ride on the mother's back for about a week until they moult. During this time the female wolf spider continues to run, hunt, and burrow, and the spiderlings must hold on. Once they leave their mother, the young wolf spiders live solitary lives. The initial protection given to the eggs and spiderlings undoubtedly contributes to the survival success of the wolf spiders.

The Mound Maker

Scattered everywhere throughout the Great Sand Hills are numerous small mounds of sand that seem to lack a maker. There are no animals running about, and no holes can be seen. The mounds often occur in groups and may form a straight line; sometimes they are linked together by a rope of elevated earth. The mounds are often mistakenly attributed to moles, but there are no moles in the grasslands. The mysterious mounds are the work of the secretive northern pocket gopher. The pocket gopher is not to be confused with the Richardson ground squirrel which is also commonly called a gopher. Although both the ground squirrel and the pocket gopher are rodents that live in burrows, the ground squirrel spends much of its time aboveground and is frequently seen, whereas the pocket gopher rarely leaves its burrow.

I have seen a live pocket gopher only once but I have examined museum specimens a number of times. Pocket gophers, which are a little smaller than ground squirrels, are grayish brown rodents with short, naked tails, and body features that are well adapted to tunnelling. They have large shoulders and strong front limbs equipped with long, curved claws for digging. The toes of the forepaws have fringes of hair that presumably increase the effectiveness of the foot as a shovel. The skin of the pocket gopher is loose and enables the animal to move about easily in the confinement of its burrow, and it is covered with silky fur to which particles of soil do not adhere. Common to many animals that live underground, the pocket gopher has very small eyes and tiny, external ears.

The animal derives its name from a pair of external, fur-lined cheek pouches that extend along either side of its neck and open at the sides of its mouth. The gopher uses these pockets to carry food and bedding material.

In its search for food, the solitary pocket gopher digs an extensive network of subterranean tunnels. They feed mainly on moist roots and tubers, and sometimes they will pull an entire plant down through the surface soil into their burrow. The characteristic mounds are formed when the animals tunnel to the surface and push up the surplus soil. In a year a pocket gopher will push up 30-50 mounds and excavate almost a ton of earth.

Many grassland animals dig or live in burrows, but the pocket gopher is the only one that plugs the entrance to its burrow with soil so that it is largely cut off from the outside air. Thus, the animal creates a closed microenvironment. The pocket gopher benefits from the resultant high humidity (85-95%) within its closed system of tunnels, and it can maintain water balance just with the moisture in its food. Although the closed system of tunnels minimizes the animal's need for water, other stresses are imposed. The level of oxygen may be quite low and the buildup of carbon dioxide, which the animal exhales in normal respiration, may be very high. Concentrations of carbon dioxide as high as 60 times that of atmospheric air have been recorded. The pocket gopher can deal with low concentrations of oxygen because of its slow rate of metabolism, but it is still unexplained how the animal endures such high levels of carbon dioxide, which are normally considered lethal.

The pocket gopher is found throughout the mixed grasslands, especially in regions where the soil is loose and easy to excavate. In agricultural areas it is considered a pest, particularly where alfalfa is grown, since it not only consumes the plant but its mounds make it more difficult to harvest the crop. To the farmer, this animal may seem worthless but with its activities the pocket gopher enhances the aeration and moisture retention of the soil and it also helps to build new soil by bringing fresh subsoil to the surface.

Animal Signals

It has been said that communication in humans is 80% nonverbal, yet we place relatively little significance on anything other than language. In other animals the emphasis in communication is on postural, tactile, and olfactory signals, as well as some minor vocal cues. In the Great Sand Hills, rodents are both plentiful and diverse, and two of them, the porcupine and the deer mouse, illustrate how other animals communicate.

For most of the year the porcupine is a silent loner spending its days hidden in clumps of brush or in an earthen den; it comes out only at night, to feed on the small twigs, tender buds, and inner bark of willows and aspen. In October and November love is in the air, and it is the time to whimper, whine, rub and cohabit. The potential mating period in porcupines is relatively short. The female is in heat for only 8-12 hours. Under these circumstances the female porcupine is frequently the one to initiate courtship by moaning and rubbing noses with her intended mate to ensure that he gets the point. The idea of porcupine love inevitably launches one on flights of fantasy and conjecture, considering that every porcupine is armed with an arsenal of 30,000 quills. But copulation proceeds in a familiar way, after the female flattens the quills on her back and twists her tail to the side. Afterwards, one animal typically waddles off. If the other animal follows with further amorous intent the first one screams its displeasure. The rejected lover has no recourse and trots off resigned to being loved and left.

The deer mouse, the most abundant mammal in the Great Sand Hills, uses different signals to communicate. The deer mouse is primarily nocturnal, and it lives close to the ground where vegetation is thick. Both of these factors preclude, to a great extent, the use of visual signals in communication. Vocal signalling would be hazardous since it would alert predators, so deer mice are not highly vocal. But mice need to transmit the same messages as do larger mammals. They must communicate sex, social status, age, reproductive condition, alarm, aggression, greetings, submission, territorial occupancy, and family membership. The sense of smell is well developed in mammals, and in small mammals, like the mouse, odour signals, called *pheromones*, play the most important role in communication.

In the deer mouse it has been shown that pheromones exert a remarkable influence on the animal's metabolism and can affect and accelerate reproductive development. In one intriguing experiment female deer mice were isolated from male mice. Within a short time the reproductive cycles of the females were affected, and they began to ovulate less frequently. When as little as 0.2 milliliters of adult male urine was dripped into the cages of the females, it stimulated ovulation in almost all the female mice. Hence, the presence of the male animal was unnecessary, and only his odour was important to bring females into reproductive readiness. In another study of small rodents related to the deer mouse, one group of female mice was reared with male mice and another group was reared alone. The females reared with males reached sexual maturity twenty days earlier than those reared without males. The same study was repeated, but the second time the male's urine was used instead of the male, and it still produced precocious development in the females. The effect of pheromones on male development was also tested, and, predictably, it was shown that the odour of female mice accelerated the development of the testes in young male mice. All of these experiments were conducted on caged animals and we cannot assume that similar mechanisms operate in the wild, although it is tempting to speculate, since the ecological advantages of such synchronizing and accelerating factors are obvious.

A final dramatic example will illustrate the importance that odour signals play in the lives of mice. A pregnant female mouse was separated from her mate within five days of being impregnated. She was then caged with a strange male, one from a different population of mice. The female quickly aborted and immediately came into heat again. The same sequence occurred when only the urine of the strange male was used. Once again these results were obtained in a laboratory setting, but one can speculate that, should a similar mechanism operate in the wild, it would be an effective way to protect against inbreeding and would lead to more genetic diversity, a circumstance that unquestionably enhances the survival of the species.

Sand reed grass is a pioneering species. In association with sand dropseed and Indian rice grass, it is one of the earliest grasses to secure a foothold on barren sand dunes. By stabilizing the sand it sets the stage for the establishment of less hardy grasses.

Over the last 10,000 years there have been ten periods of aridity in the Great Sand Hills of Saskatchewan. All of these periods of drought produced dune movement.

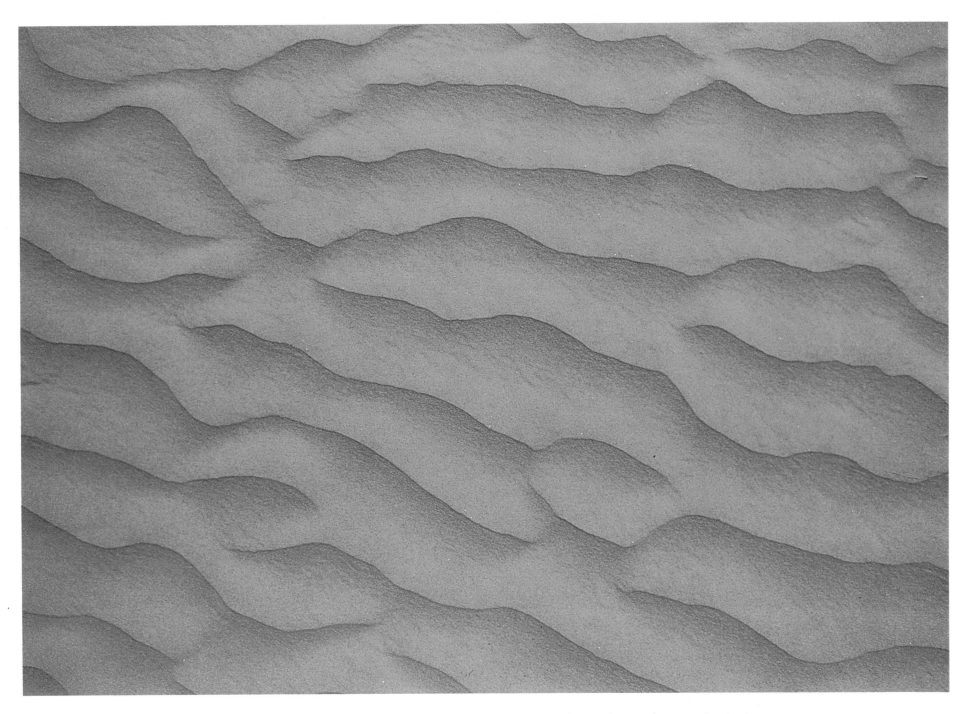

Ripples form on the surface of a dune at right angles to the wind. The distance between the ripples is the average distance that a grain of sand hops ahead when it is lifted by the wind.

The deer mouse is a prolific breeder. It has 2-4 litters a year, and each litter commonly contains 4-6 young. The young can breed at 5-6 weeks of age.

The wings of the swallowtail butterfly are completely covered with tiny, flat scales, arranged in overlapping rows. As well as normal scales, special scent scales occur along the rear edge of the hindwing of male swallowtails.

As well as its quills, the porcupine has a woolly undercoat and long, coarse guard hairs. The guard hairs conceal the quills until the animal is aroused. The quills are longest on the shoulders and back, and when raised they push the guard hairs forward to form a crest. Each hollow quill tapers to a point closely covered by several dozen small barbs. Lost quills are continually replaced.

The snowy owl is a winter migrant to the mixed grasslands.

The white-tailed jackrabbit is actually a hare, not a rabbit, and as with all hares, it is born fully furred and with its eyes open. All hares in Canada turn white in winter.

The nighthawk is not a hawk at all but a member of the goatsucker family that includes the familiar whip-poor-will and a rare grassland bird called the poor-will. All of these birds are soft-feathered and have long, pointed wings and short, weak legs and feet. They have very small bills but a wide gaping mouth. Their flight is strong, erratic and batlike, and they feed on flies, mosquitoes and moths caught on the wing.

Formerly the swift fox ranged in the mixed grasslands from the foothills of the Rocky Mountains to the Pembina Hills in Manitoba, but it was last seen in the wild in the 1930's. It is currently being reintroduced into the three prairie provinces.

Trees may do well in sand if they are able to grow their roots deep enough to reach the water table.

Eight to twelve grouse comprise a typical group on a dancing ground throughout most of the bird's range. The central position of the dancing grounds is held by the socially dominant birds. The grouse inflate a violet pouch on the side of their neck as part of their dancing display.

The "tail rattling" display of the male grouse is one of the most interesting displays. The tail is cocked and the white underfeathers are exposed and expanded for maximum visibility. The wings are outstretched and the head held low, and in this posture the male runs forward with rapid stepping movements. At the same time he vibrates his tail from side to side to produce a scraping noise as the tail feathers overlap.

81

The tarsal scent gland of this mule deer can be seen as a dark spot on the inside of its rear leg. Secretions from this gland advertise the individual identity of an animal. The mule deer has additional scent glands between its toes, on the lower parts of its legs, and associated with its mouth, eyes and anus.

The Canada anemone is a member of the Buttercup Family.

The large eyes of the wolf spider permit it to hunt by vision rather than relying on a silken web to trap its prey.

The male floral parts (stamens) of the goatsbeard blossom are laden with pollen. The female floral parts (pistils) are in the center of the blossom. Frequently, the stamens and pistils of flowers mature at different times to prevent self pollination.

The visual acuity of a hawk's eyes is legendary, and their resolving power is based on several features. The large size of their eyes produces a large image on their retina, which is densely packed with visual cells. In the human retina there can be 200,000 visual cells to each square millimeter whereas in a large hawk, such as the rough legged hawk pictured, there are as many as 1,000,000 visual cells to each square millimeter, making the hawk's vision superior to man's.

The colours of feathers are derived either from pigments or from the optical effects of light on the microscopic structure of the feather. White, blue and green feathers are optical illusions caused by the structure of the feather. Black, brown, orange, yellow and the vibrant red breast feathers of the ring-necked pheasant derive their colour from pigments.

The red-tailed hawk is a heavy-bodied hawk that nests in coulees, and hunts by soaring over open country.

The dried seed pods of Frenchweed.

Layers of Time

Some believe that the early French explorers to the prairies coined the name badlands because the regions were difficult to traverse. Others contest that the name has a more recent origin, and that it was applied by early settlers who found the land impossible to farm. Whichever you believe, the badlands are still only "bad" from the viewpoint of man. Within the mixed grass prairie the badlands are a separate habitat attracting their own flora and fauna, and possessed of their own beauty, enticing in its ruggedness.

The Blackfoot Indians came to the badlands to dream and seek visions, and outlaws came to hide from the noose. Within the deep valleys of the badlands the fossils of dinosaurs erupt from clay slopes, and in mid-July, when the heat is paralyzing, the land then seems to have only its past, for nothing stirs. The badlands are one of my favorite haunts. In the badlands I drift and wander, for to introduce a pace or a purpose would lessen the experience. There I have found secret nooks where I have rested and reflected on man's place in the grasslands. Man is the product of 4½ billion years of fortuitous events, the culmination of evolution. But there is nothing that suggests that the evolutionary process has stopped. Man is a transitional animal. We will pass as our countless ancestors have passed. The badlands console me, and they reaffirm my belief in the necessity of change and the perserverance of life.

Badlands — What, When, Where and Why

A typical tract of badlands is all up and down. It consists of a landscape extensively dissected by steep, narrow valleys, the slopes of which are relatively free of vegetation, revealing multi-coloured layers of bedrock. Most of the bedrock that surfaces in the prairies, excluding the superficial glacial deposits, is sedimentary rock from the Cretaceous Period. During the late Cretaceous Period a successive series of large inland seas, the last of which was called the Bearpaw Sea, occupied the central basin of North America, including the Canadian mixed grasslands region. At one point the Bearpaw Sea was immense and stretched between the Arctic Ocean and the Gulf of Mexico. The size and shorelines of these seas were variable over the millions of years of their existence, until the last sea finally disappeared with the general continental uplift of central North America, approximately 65 million years ago. During this time innumerable great rivers carrying rock fragments of all sizes from coarse gravels and sands to finer clays and silts, emptied into the inland seas from the uplands of the Canadian Shield in the east and the mountains in the west, and dumped their cargo of sediments. The larger, heavier sediments settled first; later they became compacted into conglomerates and coarse and fine sandstones. The fine clays and silts settled farther out from shore and became beds of siltstones and shales. Because of the nature of their deposition all sedimentary rocks are layered, arranged in successive beds one on top of the other. If a sequence of beds has not been disturbed (by tectonic activity, for example) the layers at the bottom are the oldest, with increasingly younger layers on top. The rock layers differ in colour and texture, dependent upon their sediment composition and the parent rocks from which the sediments originated. The various layers of sedimentary rock are called *formations*, and each has a name. Three of these formations, the Edmonton, Oldman, and Bearpaw formations, are particularly notable because of their rich endowment of dinosaur fossils.

During the Cretaceous Period, volcanoes occasionally erupted in areas adjacent to the mixed grassland region and covered it with volcanic ash. The volcanic ash was altered by weathering and was transformed into bentonite, a clay with highly absorbent qualities. Bentonite clay is found in a number of prairie geological formations, and it is mined commercially at Truax, south of Regina. The clay has diverse uses ranging from drilling muds to its use as a bulking agent in cosmetics and toothpaste. Slopes containing bentonite have a characteristic appearance when they dry out after a rainfall; the surface cracks and forms crumbly chunks that resemble popcorn.

The layer of icing is all that you see before you remove a slice from a chocolate layer cake. The image holds for the sedimentary layers of bedrock that underlie the mixed grass prairie. Unless something cuts into the bedrock, only the youngest layer on top is visible. The greatest enemy of rock is running water, and when rivers are heavily laden with sediments, it adds to their bite, and the water eats into bedrock. In the mixed grasslands, former glacial meltwater channels and rivers have cut deeply into the bedrock, exposing the layers of time and creating the badland topography.

In Saskatchewan, badlands flank the Big Muddy, Morgan, and Frenchman Rivers, and in Alberta the shoulders of the Milk River valley have been sculpted into badlands that are like no others. The most spectacular badlands parallel the banks of the Red Deer River, especially near Drumheller, Alberta, and in Dinosaur Provincial Park. Dinosaur Provincial Park is internationally recognized as the world's most important dinosaur fossil field and as a landscape of unique physical character. In 1979 the park was named to the list of World Heritage Sites by the United Nations Educational, Scientific, and Cultural Organization (UNESCO) in recognition of its outstanding universal value.

Badlands were created by the action of running water, and today the forces of erosion continue. The English language is full of expressions extolling the permanency of rock. Yet rocks everywhere, especially the relatively soft sedimentary rocks of the badlands, are slowly and continually dissolved by chemical action, and are attacked by wind driven ice and grit that abrades their surfaces like sandpaper. The recurrent cycle of freezing and thawing can chip and fracture even the hardest rocks. But the true architect of erosion is water, as rain, runoff, hail or sleet. Water expands 10% in

volume when it freezes. This expansion exerts an immense force within cracks. The products of all of this erosion are pinnacles, buttes and hoodoos, the dramatic landforms of the badlands.

The rock layers of the badlands vary in hardness, and thus vary in their susceptibility to erosion. Harder layers persist longer, and sometimes when they overlie softer layers, hoodoos are formed. These are columns of rock topped by hard protective caprocks. The Indians feared hoodoos, believing them to be petrified giants who came alive at night and hurled rocks at intruders. Bentonite clay weathers more rapidly than sandstone, and when the softer bentonite forms the upper layer, rounded mounds and "turtlebacks" are produced. Sandstone erodes into sharper outlines and steeper slopes. The forces of erosion are leveling Dinosaur Provincial Park by a centimeter a year. This is an exceptionally rapid rate of erosion if you compare it to the erosion rate in the Rocky Mountains which is only a centimeter every 1000 years. It is estimated that the Dinosaur Park badlands will be flattened in 10,000 years.

Erosion occurs not only on the surface of the badlands but also within. The erosion within forms a system of caves and piping channels. Scientists have released smoke bombs within the caves and watched where the smoke exits to determine the extensiveness of the piping system. The badlands are being eaten away inside and out, and carried away in rivers. After every rain a little more of the slopes are washed away. The badlands originated from sediments washed in by extinct rivers, and now the badlands are being washed away by today's rivers to form new beds of sediments that may, in millions of years, be exposed again. It is a recurrent cycle. But as the badlands are stripped away fossils are exposed, and each year the agents of erosion deliver more remnants from the past for paleontologists to ponder.

The Petrified Past

Webster's dictionary defines a fossil as "a remnant, impression, or trace of an animal or plant of past geological ages that has been preserved in the earth's crust." A fossil can be a footprint, the outline of a leaf, skin impressions, a bone or tooth, a shell, stomach stones or petrified dung. Generally, if a structure is to become fossilized it must be first rapidly buried by sediments. Then groundwater slowly seeps into all of the cells and spaces of the animal or plant. Minerals, such as, silica, calcite and pyrite, that are in the water, slowly replace, molecule by molecule, the parts of the wood, bone or shell and form a replica of the original. At other times the structure is simply buried quickly with sediment that solidifies, and later, when the original structure decomposes and disappears, a mould is left. The mould may then fill with minerals, and a perfect cast is formed.

The most notable fossils to be found in the badlands are those of dinosaurs. The Age of the Dinosaurs began about 200 million years ago in the middle of the Triassic Period and dinosaurs flourished for 130 million years. Dinosaurs were grazers, browsers, egg eaters, meat eaters and scavengers; some were as small as the iguanas of today and others, like the Albertosaurus, were 15 meters long and weighed more than a hundred people. A number of the predaceous dinosaurs walked upright on massive hind limbs. To supply these limbs with nerves, the terminal part of the animal's spinal cord was greatly enlarged, several times the size of its brain, and this led many to believe that the dinosaur had two brains.

Behold the mighty dinosaur
Famous in prehistoric lore,
Not only for his power and strength
But for his intellectual length.
You will observe by these remains
The creature had two sets of brains —
One in his head (the usual place),
The other at his spinal base.
Thus he could reason "A priori"
As well as "A posteriori."
No problem bothered him a bit
He made both head and tail of it.
So wise was he, so wise and solemn,
Each thought filled just a spinal column.

If one brain found the pressure strong
It passed a few ideas along.
If something slipped his forward mind
'Twas rescued by the one behind.
And if in error he was caught
He had a saving afterthought.
As he thought twice before he spoke
He had no judgement to revoke.
Thus he could think without congestion
Upon both sides of every question.
Oh gaze upon this model beast,
Defunct 10 million years at least.

Bert Taylor
Chicago Tribune 1912

Dinosaur remains have been found on all of the continents and, to date, at least four dozen species of dinosaurs have been uncovered from the Cretaceous deposits in the badlands of the mixed grass prairie. At the end of the Cretaceous Period the dinosaurs were flourishing in variety and in numbers, and then suddenly they were gone. Not one dinosaur skeleton has been found in the deposits of the Tertiary Period, which came after the Cretaceous Period.

The Dinosaurs Disappear

Nothing can quite match the unfettered enthusiasm mustered by scientists in their early attempts to explain the extinction of the dinosaur. Overcrowding and a drop in global temperatures were popular theories used to explain the disappearance. Competition from the newly evolved mammals also seemed plausible, as well as mammalian predation on dinosaur eggs. A few suggested that the newly evolving flowering plants of the late Cretaceous Period produced toxic alkaloids that poisoned the dinosaurs. But the funniest explanation is the one that postulates that flowering plants were indigestible to dinosaurs and they died of constipation.

The dinosaurs of the Cretaceous Period tended to be the

largest. Greater size brought with it the problems of slower movement, greater food requirements, and longer development of the young. All of these factors make animals vulnerable to change, accident and disease. The dinosaurs were not the only animals to suddenly disappear 63 million years ago. Seventy-five percent of all the animals and plants of the world disappeared along with the dinosaur. In recent years an intriguing explanation has been proposed that may be the final answer.

Floating through space are countless fragments of rocks, remnants from the formation of the solar system. Scientists postulate that one of these fragments, an asteroid ten kilometers in diameter, and travelling 65,000 kilometers/hour, collided with the earth. The asteroid would have vapourized on impact, throwing a thick dust cloud into the atmosphere and blocking out the sun. The cloud, swept along by the jet stream, would have quickly circled the entire earth. This theory is supported by a layer of clay found in the rocks from the late Cretaceous Period in New Zealand, Denmark and Italy. These rocks contain unusual levels of iridium, as much as 160 times the normal trace amounts. Iridium is rare in the rocks of the earth, but relatively abundant in asteroids. The asteroidal impact would have blocked the sun for three to five years, shutting down photosynthesis, disrupting plant growth and interrupting the food chain. Plant-eating animals would have died first, followed by predators, and finally scavengers.

The record of the mass extinctions that ended the Cretaceous Period shows certain anomalies. For example, land plants of the northern regions of the Temperate Zone suffered more losses than land plants farther south. But freshwater plants and animals of both northern and southern regions were scarcely affected. In another instance, no land animal weighing more than 25 kilograms survived, yet many of the ones that disappeared were considerably smaller. Clearly, the asteroidal impact theory still leaves many questions unanswered, but until it can be discredited it remains the final word.

Outlaws and Pilgrims

The badlands played a role in the lives of many men. In the 1880's outlaw gangs lived in caves of the Big Muddy Badlands of southern Saskatchewan and they terrorized the region. At that time a drought had gripped the American Plains and cattle died, ranches folded and cowboys were set adrift, jobless and without a home. Many of these cowhands drifted north into the Montana-Saskatchewan country. Out of this migration sprang a tough, lawless gang of rowdies and rustlers called The Wild Bunch. The American West might have had Jesse James, Billy the Kid and the Daltons, but the Wild Bunch included such notorious disreputables as Dutch Henry, The Pigeon-Toed Kid, Bloody Knife, and the Nelson Gang, miscreants that all became legendary figures. Though train and bank robberies were included among their dastardly deeds, the stock-in-trade of the Wild Bunch was rustling livestock. The gang, hiding out in the Big Muddy, would regularly sneak across the border to steal horses and cattle. The livestock was herded back across the border into Canada, the brands "adjusted," and the animals sold. These same animals were often stolen again and taken back to the Dakotas and Montana to be sold once more. The ranchers on both sides of the border were continually threatened, and they lived in constant fear of reprisals.

Befitting their lifestyle, many of the Wild Bunch members came to a colourful end. Bloody Knife was killed in a drunken brawl, and an angry posse convinced the Pigeon-Toed Kid to hang around for a while. Others were shot by American lawmen or ended their days in prison cells. Sam Kelly, believed to be the leader of the gang, died in North Battleford, Saskatchewan, in 1954, alone and in obscurity.

For the Indians of the plains, the badlands were a sacred place. The Indians believed that the world was charged with supernatural importance, and that all natural phenomena, mountains, rivers, waterfalls and cliffs were manifestations of spirits and were sacred. It is easy to understand how the mounds and hoodoos of the badlands acquired a reputation as a place of powerful spirits.

Writing-On-Stone Provincial Park in the Milk River badlands of southern Alberta is the site of one of the largest collections of prehistoric rock art in North America. Thousands of petroglyphs and a few rock paintings, petrographs, grace the sandstone cliffs of the park badlands. The scenes depicted are of men with shields and weapons, and of elk, bison, bears, horses, snakes and birds. The area has been part of the religious beliefs and practices of native peoples for 3000 years. For them the badlands were a sacred place to be respected and feared, where spirits wrote on the rocks. Indian men came to Writing-On-Stone to seek advice from their guardian spirits. Before entering the valley they would select a high point, build a fire of sweetgrass, and inhale the smoke to purify themselves. Afterwards, they would fast for days, and through their dreams and the inspiration derived from the petroglyphs the men could learn of the future. A man could add his own inscriptions, but only if he received instructions in a vision. The visions contained secret knowledge from which the dreamer obtained his power.

Rock art is found in other mixed grassland regions, in Saskatchewan near Estevan and Assiniboia, and in Montana near Billings. The Plains Indians believed that the acts of carving and painting were a means of acquiring power, and regaining control over their environment, and since they were subject to the vicissitudes of nature, such beliefs may have been their only defense against despair. Like most men today, the Plains Indians were sustained by their faith.

Snake Pit

Snakes cannot withstand freezing temperatures, so in Canada all species must hibernate during the winter. They hibernate in dens located below the frost line, and in the badlands the deeper crevices and piping systems provide access to suitable depths where winter temperatures are much less severe. Although the badlands are filled with crevices, probably only a few are suitable as winter dens, so several species of snakes will often den together. One such den I frequently census shelters garter snakes, yellow-bellied racers, bullsnakes and prairie rattlesnakes.

Snakes evolved in the tropics, and their survival in seasonally cold climates has demanded certain adaptations. The red-sided garter snake occurs father north than any other snake in North America, and so the details of its life history have attracted great attention, in an effort to understand how reptiles survive in cold environments.

Red-sided garter snakes hibernate for eight months of the year. During the remaining four months, when they leave the den, they must feed, grow, produce their young and accumulate enough fat to survive the lengthy winter hibernation. It is therefore advantageous for the red-sided garter snake, and probably all other grassland snakes, to overwinter in groups, so that no time is wasted in spring searching for mating partners. Some red-sided garter snake dens contain 10,000-15,000 snakes, the greatest aggregation of snakes to occur anywhere on earth.

The garter snakes emerge from hibernation in late April and early May. The males are the first to appear and they surface in great numbers. Soon after, over a period of several weeks, the females start to surface, one by one or in small groups. The staggered, delayed emergence of the female garter snakes as opposed to the early, mass emergence of the male snakes may have survival value. With the ratio of males to females around the den entrance as high as 50 to 1, the probability of females being fertilized is virtually 100 percent. Also important to consider is that if all the females were to emerge together, mate, and disperse early in the season, unpredictable freezing temperatures might destroy much of the breeding population. The intermittent emergence of the females insures that some will survive.

As soon as a female emerges from the den she is mobbed by male suitors. "Mating balls" are formed, consisting of a single female intertwined with dozens of males. Mating balls attract males from all directions. At times the males will even chase females up into bushes and small trees. A mating ball usually contains thirty snakes or less but as many as a hundred have been recorded. The female is cold and torpid when she first emerges and her sluggishness probably works to the advantage of the courting males.

The male courtship urge is very strong. In experiments, males will even court dead females. This illustrates that the active role of the female garter snake in courtship is minor, if anything. In the laboratory, male garter snakes refuse to eat during the initial mating period, but after three or four weeks, as the courtship urge wanes, the snake's appetite returns. The temporary suppression of appetite, which undoubtedly also occurs in the wild, helps the species to survive. In the grasslands, red-sided garter snakes hibernate for most of the year and they are in a state of near starvation when they emerge in the spring. Logically, the snakes would be expected to leave the den immediately and seek food. The initial lack of appetite helps to keep male snakes at the den during the mating period. In this instance, reproduction and perpetuation of the species takes precedence over the nutrition and survival of the individual.

Male snakes find newly emerging females extremely attractive. A pheromone released through the skin is responsible for the female's magnetism. Courting males detect the pheromone with their tongue-flicking. Often on first contact the male will drape his tongue over the female's back. The skin between the scales of her back is extremely thin and has a rich, underlying network of blood vessels that brings the pheromone close to the surface.

Copulation lasts 15-20 minutes. The males possess two intromittent organs called *hemipenes* — hollow, cylindrical bodies that retract into cavities in the base of the tail. Only a single hemipenis is used at a time. After mating the male leaves a gelatinous plug in the female's orifice and it serves somewhat as a chastity belt. The copulatory plug contains a different pheromone, one that inhibits male courtship behaviour so that attention is focused on the unmated females and the mated females are spared repeated mating attempts, thus minimizing the energy expended in mating at a time when their energy reserves are particularly low. Females leave the den site as soon as they have mated and disperse to summer feeding marshes. The young are born there in late August.

Most reptiles lay eggs, but the red-sided garter snake gives birth to live young. When these and others such as the red-bellied snake, rattlesnake, and short-horned lizard bear live young the eggs are retained within the body of the female and are warmed and incubated each time she basks, improving the odds of successful hatching. If eggs were laid and left to develop on their own they would be vulnerable to destruction by cold summer conditions.

By early autumn the fat reserves of the garter snakes are high from a summer of feeding, and they return to the den for another eight months. By late October all of the snakes have disappeared underground.

The Black Widow

Within a day of her capture the spider had spun a disorganized sheet of webbing, and she spent her time hanging beneath the web, the scarlet hourglass on her abdomen advertising her identity. Pound for pound, she was the most dangerous animal I had ever photographed. I knew that no one in Canada had ever died from the bite of a black widow spider, but I wasn't sure if the spider knew that, and having her as a pet was an exhilarating experience. One morning her abdomen was markedly shrunken and she had spun a globular silken egg case. For weeks after that she was always beside her eggs, and left them only to feed on the dead house flies that I provided. After five weeks there was a tiny hole in the egg sac, and the web was sprinkled with 49 white and brown spiderlings. In the wild, adult females die shortly after their eggs hatch, and the young disperse to spend the winter alone. My spiders now live in drawer No. 674 of the invertebrate collection of the Saskatchewan Museum of Natural History.

The handsome black widow spider is found in a number of locations in Canada, including the arid grassland regions of southern Alberta and southwestern Saskatchewan where they build their webs in badland cavities or abandoned rodent burrows.

Male black widows are much smaller than adult females (about 1/10 the size) and are not black, but patterned with grey, tan and orange. Prior to mating the male spider spins a tiny sperm web upon which he deposits a globule of semen. The copulatory organs of spiders look like boxing gloves at the end of two short appendages located beside the spider's head. The male dips the boxing gloves, called *pedipalps*, into the globule of semen and fills them with sperm. He is now ready to seek a female.

Unlike the wolf spider, which uses vision to locate both its mate and its prey, the black widow is a web-builder and relies on web vibrations to signal the approach of a mate. The male spider cautiously approaches the edge of the female's web and plucks out a vibratory message identifying himself to her. The predatory habit of spiders makes recognition of the sexual partner especially important. The webbing of the black widow spider contains a pheromone that identifies her to the male. If she is receptive the male approaches and manoeuvers his pedipalps into apposition with her genital openings on the underside of her abdomen, and sperm are transferred. Afterwards, the male usually, but not always, lingers on the female's web and she eats him. The common name "black widow" refers to this interesting reproductive strategy that has evolved in the animal. If the male spider were not eaten it would normally die soon after mating anyway. By consuming her mate, the female black widow capitalizes on an opportunity to obtain nutrients that are necessary to successfully complete egg laying. Outside the world of man there is no right and wrong, only the pressing need to survive.

The Hunters and the Hunted

I was well into my adult life when I realized a very obvious natural principle, namely, that there is order in the scheme of life, and that everything has a reason and a strategy. Such is the case when you consider the energy budgets of different diurnal birds of prey.

Within the badlands there are four resident birds of prey, the turkey vulture, the ferruginous hawk, the golden eagle, and the prairie falcon, and they are able to coexist with minimal competition because each bird selects prey that matches its energy budget. Of the four birds of prey the turkey vulture has the largest wing surface area per kilogram of body weight; thus it expends the least amount of energy to stay aloft. Because it is a scavenger, eating mostly carrion, the vulture expends no energy in subduing its prey. Balancing the turkey vulture's low energy requirements is the relative scarcity of carrion. Thus predator and prey are perfectly matched. Only a bird that uses very little energy to hunt could survive primarily on carrion.

The ferruginous hawk hunts by soaring but is unable to use air currents as efficiently as the vulture because of a smaller wing surface. The hawk, therefore, expends more energy in hunting. The ferruginous hawk feeds on small rodents. Small rodents are more plentiful than carrion, and can be captured more easily. Thus the greater energy supply needed by the ferruginous hawk is offset by the more plentiful and relatively accessible food supply.

The golden eagle is large enough to prey on rabbits and hares, and a successful hunt yields a large amount of food. But in contrast to carrion and small rodents, rabbits and hares are alert, swift, have sharp eyes and good reflexes, and are armed with sharp teeth and claws to defend themselves. To prey on these animals, eagles must soar and locate the prey, then use a low level, screened approach, often terminating with rapid flapping pursuit. Once they grab the animal it may take considerable energy to subdue it, and then more energy is expended tearing up the prey into bites they can swallow. Although the food package is larger, it costs a lot more in terms of energy.

Finally, there is the prairie falcon. Like all falcons, the prairie falcon has relatively small, pointed wings that enable it to attain great speeds, but the trade-off is a higher energy consumption. The prairie falcon will sometimes use gravity to increase its speed without increasing the energy cost. In this instance, the bird climbs to a certain height and then dives with fixed wings. The prairie falcon feeds on keen-sighted birds — doves and larks — so speed is advantageous; but the prairie falcon is able to balance its energy budget because larks and doves are plentiful in the badlands, and easy to subdue.

Hot Enough to Fry an Egg

Vegetation is scanty over much of the badlands, with clumps of creeping juniper, greasewood, rabbitbrush and sagebrush scattered here and there. Grasses and clumps of snowberry and prairie rose grow in the bottoms of ravines, where there is less erosion and where runoff collects to provide more moisture. But for the most part, the badlands are naked slopes of clay and sandstone that shimmer in the summer heat. I carry a thermometer when I hike, and once, when I placed it on a clay slope of the badlands, the mercury went past 50°C and off the end of the column. The clay slopes of the badlands are a harsh, severe microhabitat, the ultimate test of animal adaptability. Dozens of birds nest in the badlands, but only the nighthawk makes its nest on the open ground where unprotected eggs can fry within minutes.

The nighthawk protects its eggs on the hot, bare ground of the badlands by incubating them constantly. Thus the temperature of the eggs approximates the body temperature of the parent, despite the higher ambient temperature. While sitting on their eggs and protecting them from the heat, parent nighthawks are subjected to intense solar radiation, and risk having their own body temperature rise. Like all birds and mammals, the nighthawk must maintain its body temperature within strict, narrow limits. The nighthawk stays cool by evaporation from the lining of its mouth. The bird's deceptively tiny beak belies an enormous gape which opens up to its ears. When the bird begins to overheat it opens it mouth, presenting a large, moist surface for evaporation. The lining of the bird's mouth is richly vascularized which further facilitates the dissipation of heat. If this measure is insufficient to maintain the bird's normal body temperature of 40-41°C, then the nighthawk vibrates its throat, rapidly passing air back and forth, which can lower the body temperature within 30 seconds.

An ingenious experiment showed that the adult nighthawk treats its eggs as extensions of its own body. In the study, the nighthawk's eggs were replaced by plastic replicas that contained a heating coil. When the investigators increased the temperature of the artificial eggs the adult bird responded by opening its mouth and fluttering its throat, using the same cooling device that it uses to protect its own body from overheating.

"Nature abhors a vaccuum," and in each of the grassland habitats we have seen that animals fill every niche, and they survive by individual blends of behavior and structure. The endless ingenuity of life defies total comprehension, and it is the infinity of design that maintains my wonder.

The swift-flying prairie falcon feeds principally on other birds, such as horned larks, mourning doves and meadowlarks.

The landscape of Dinosaur Provincial Park, in Alberta, has been sculptured by the elements. Rainfall has etched the surface with fissures called rills.

After mating, the female black widow spider commonly prepares one to three large egg sacs, each containing 150-600 eggs. Over the course of a day the egg sacs are moved as often as twice an hour to take advantage of the most favourable sunlight and temperature conditions. Every evening, and when it rains, the egg sacs are moved inside.

The male lark sparrow courts the female by strutting on the ground with its wings trailing and its tail spread, showing the white corners.

The blooms of the pincushion cactus are among the most brilliant in the grasslands. Like all cactus, the pincushion lacks leaves, which long ago evolved into clusters of spines.

The prickly pear cactus blooms over an extended period from mid June to July. Its fruit is a sweet, edible berry about 2.5 centimeters long that can be made into a delicious jam.

Despite its name, the mountain bluebird occurs as commonly in the grasslands as it does in the mountains. This adult male is delivering a grasshopper to its family of nestlings hidden in a crevice in the badlands.

The moss phlox is one of the earliest flowers to bloom in the grasslands. It hugs the ground, rarely growing more than 2.5 centimeters high, in a dense cluster of leaves where temperatures may be many degrees warmer than the air above.

The short horned lizard can grow up to 120 mm long, including its tail. It has foregone laying eggs in underground nests, as the cool temperatures of the soil throughout the Canadian mixed grasslands would not permit development of the embryos. Instead it gives birth to live young.

The prickly pear cactus is well adapted to heat and aridity: it stores moisture in its succulent stems; its roots course close to the surface to soak up the slightest shower; its spines shade the plant and also protect it from grazing animals; and it conducts photosynthesis at night when the humidity is highest and water loss minimal.

The bobcat is a solitary hunter. Hares and rabbits make up the bulk of its diet, followed by various rodents, birds and insects. In spring it may also take fawns and pronghorn kids.

The nonpoisonous yellow-bellied racer is a slender, fast-moving snake of the coulees and hillsides. A good climber, it will often sun on the branches of shrubs, and it can glide over the tops of bushes almost as quickly as if it were on the ground.

Silver sagebrush is abundant in the lowlands of Dinosaur Provincial Park. The park is a World Heritage Site, so designated for its rich fossil deposits and dramatic badland scenery.

Coulees

Autumn is my favorite season. Cool days, waning daylight, and geese overhead create an air of gentle melancholy as the greens of summer are touched with scarlet, gold and orange. I remember most vividly an October day when I explored a coulee near Eastend, Saskatchewan. It was bitterly cold and a strong wind muscled its way out of the northwest, numbing my cheeks, but I felt ablaze with life. The land was in full conversation with the wind, and the whisper of leaves and chatter of branches was often interrupted by the cries and groans of bending trunks. The air was rich and heavy with fragrance, and I inhaled deeply to taste it with my lungs. As I strolled, I chewed on a blade of grass as I often do when I feel content. Just when I thought that things could not be better I looked overhead and a prairie falcon sliced across the sky. The bird was wild, free and alive, and it symbolized how I felt.

If it can be said that there are forests within the grasslands, then these forests are called coulees. The coulee is a crowded habitat of shrubs and trees huddled within protected ravines and valleys, embracing the banks of rivers and creeks. Within a coulee there is a great variety of vegetation, determined by the depth of the valley, the steepness of the slope, the direction of the slope, and most of all by the amount of moisture in the soil. I think of coulees as the only grassland habitat with a roof. Because the vegetation has height the habitat can be viewed as three separate vertical levels, although the levels are not always distinct, and some may be absent.

The top level of the coulee is the canopy formed by the crowns of trees like aspen, cottonwood, green ash and box elder. The second level is the young trees, and shrubs like snowberry, buffaloberry and shrubby cinquefoil. On the ground level are the grasses and flowers. Each of these three levels is endowed with a different combination of sunlight, moisture, wind and temperature, which yields a different microclimate. The canopy is the harshest of the microclimates, receiving the full force of the wind and rain, and the full impact of the sun's heating rays. Lower down, conditions are less extreme. At ground level the environment is most stable with practically no wind, relatively constant temperatures and humidity, and with a minimum of sunlight in summer.

The stratification of the coulee vegetation allows a greater variety of wildlife to live in that habitat. Some animals, especially invertebrates, are associated with only a single vegetation level whereas others may range over all three levels. Mice, ground squirrels and shrews use the lowest level, while deer and porcupine feed on the shrubs and young trees. Birds are the most mobile of the wildlife of the coulee and use all three levels, but they often show a preference for a particular level. For example, ruffed grouse, thrashers and towhees scratch and forage at ground level; woodpeckers and nuthatches work the trunks of trees; vireos and warblers scour the leaves of the canopy for spiders and insects; and hawks perch and nest in the tallest trees. But the greatest variety and numbers of animals are not found in any of these levels, but within the soil. Here exists a separate community with its own herbivores, carnivores and scavengers.

Life in the Soil

Within the soil, dead leaves, old roots and stems of various coulee plants are slowly decomposed. The process may start with an earthworm ingesting some of the dead vegetation. The worm's excrement will contain part of the nutrients it has ingested in addition to bacteria from its own intestinal tract. This excrement is ingested by other soil animals which absorb some of the remaining nutrients, and add their own bacterial flora to what remains. Along the line, fungi and protozoans may also become involved in the decomposition process. After multiple ingestions, the organic matter is broken down into simple chemical compounds which can then be reabsorbed by living plants and used for growth and reproduction. When the plants die, the material is returned to the soil to start the cycle again. If the cycle is interrupted at any step the soil deteriorates. This occurs in agriculture when crops are removed from the cycle, and the nutrients must be replaced by synthetic fertilizers.

Soil animals are essential for the recycling of nutrients in the coulee. They form a complex community of predators and prey, intricately adapted to their environment. Soil animals have a highly developed sense of smell and touch. Tactile hairs cover their bodies and inform them about their world. Many of the animals that live in the deeper layers of the soil are blind. Nevertheless, they still sense light, and if exposed to light for even a brief time they become restless and move about until they find a dark spot. Soil creatures also exhibit *thigmotropism*, the desire to be touched on all sides, which manifests itself in a tendency to crawl into narrow cracks and gaps in the earth.

Many soil animals, especially mites and springtails, feed on the roots of living plants. These animals are preyed upon by roundworms. In turn, various fungi prey on the roundworms, and some of the fungi are ingenious trappers. One type of fungus trap consists of a network of highly adhesive hoops which entangles the worm. A fine filament of the fungus penetrates and fills the body of the worm, absorbs its contents and leaves only the skin. Another fungus trap operates like an animal snare. The fungus has ring filaments attached to the main filament. When a roundworm passes through the ring, the friction of its body stimulates the ring cells to swell and grip the worm. The ring expansion is exceptionally rapid, one-tenth of a second, and the worm has little chance.

The soil offers protection from dessicating winds, lethal ultraviolet rays, and the extremes of temperature. But soil has a low permeability and it can dry out, flood or freeze solid. Soil animals need the same things that are needed by animals aboveground: space, oxygen, water and food. If the soil becomes saturated with water, the air within the cracks and spaces of the soil is displaced and the animals may drown. If the soil dries out or freezes, animals must either penetrate deeper or enclose themselves in a cyst or capsule and await favourable conditions.

Tick Talk

In my years of medical practise in the Emergency Department I saw people, and I saw ticks, and usually they came together. Ticks are parasites that attach themselves to the skin of animals and humans to feed on blood. Only the tick's mouthparts penetrate the skin, so it can easily be pulled loose by grasping it with a pair of tweezers. A hot needle or lighted cigarette may be applied to the tick first to relax its grip. This is a time-honoured remedy, but it requires a steady hand and is best avoided by hysterical victims.

In the grasslands there are two species of ticks that affect man: the American dog tick, and the Rocky Mountain wood tick. The dog tick is found in brushy areas, poplar groves and riversides in the eastern half of the grasslands in southeastern Saskatchewan and southern Manitoba. The wood tick, residing in the western grasslands, prefers coulees and shrub-covered hillsides, especially those inhabited by hares and ground squirrels.

Ticks are related to spiders and resemble tiny watermelon seeds with legs. Ticks have three stages in their life cycle and each stage draws blood from a different victim, and frequently the hosts are three different species of animals. In a typical life cycle the newly hatched larvae might feed on a mouse or a chipmunk; the intermediate stage, called the nymph, might suck blood from a ground squirrel or rabbit, and the adult stage might finally feed on a coyote, porcupine, deer or human. Any of the stages can overwinter in the grass and survive for a year without a meal. Adults may even survive as long as two or three years.

The adult ticks, the ones that feed on humans, are most active in the spring and persist until the end of June. They climb up into vegetation and wait for a passing animal. Ticks detect suitable prey with chemical receptors that are sensitive to carbon dioxide, the gas exhaled by all animals, and also they have thermoreceptors on their legs that detect body heat. Once the tick is on its prey it attaches itself with its mouthparts. Their salivary glands produce a cement-like substance that prevents them from being easily detached. As they may feed for ten days or more, it is important that their presence be unsuspected and ticks produce an anesthetic that makes their bite painless.

Ticks swell as they feed and although a male tick may triple his weight, the females are the true prodigious feeders. Females need blood to produce eggs and they may swell to the size of a small grape, increasing their original weight by more than a hundred times. In human terms this would be equivalent to an average woman sitting down to eat and leaving the table weighing five metric tons.

Mating occurs while the adults are still on the host. The female then drops to the ground and lays 5,000-10,000 small, brown eggs, usually in one large mass, under rocks or dried grass. The female dies afterwards. Within a month or so, depending upon the temperature, the eggs hatch into larvae that crawl up into low vegetation and await a suitable host. After they obtain a meal of blood, the six-legged larvae transform into eight-legged nymphs which must also have a blood meal to complete the transformation to adults.

Two rare human diseases have given ticks an ominous reputation. Ticks can transmit Rocky Mountain spotted fever and also produce a toxin that causes paralysis. The former is an infection characterized by headaches, chills, aching bones, muscles and joints, fever and a skin rash. Removal of the tick and antibiotic treatment normally cures the illness. Tick paralysis is caused by a toxin that acts on the spinal cord and is injected by the engorging tick. Ticks must feed for several days before symptoms develop. Removal of the tick leads to striking improvement within hours and the paralysis is completely reversible. Both of these disorders are extremely rare, and ticks should be accepted as no more than a minor annoyance. No one should forego the many rewards of wandering through a coulee for fear of ticks.

From Abundance to Bones — The Story of the Bison

The mixed grass prairie was the summer range of the bison. In autumn the animals migrated north and west out of the grasslands to spend the winter in the aspen woodlands. The bison was the mainstay of the Indians' existence, and they followed the animals wherever they moved. The Indians hunted the bison by stalking or by using communal techniques. They would drive the animals into a corral built at the rear of a steep-sided coulee, or they would herd them into deep snow where the animals became mired and were easily killed. The most successful hunting technique was the buffalo jump, a steep cliff over which bison were driven to their death. Days before a drive, the young men of the tribe would locate the bison and move the herd slowly towards the jump site, using smoke from smouldering dung. Frequently, stone cairns were built in the configuration of a funnel that led to the cliff. When the young men had the bison close enough, the animals were stampeded into the funnel. Other men hid behind the cairns and jumped up, waving and shouting to heighten the panic of the fleeing bison. The Long Creek buffalo jump, in Saskatchewan, is the oldest one in Canada, and dates from 5000 B.C. Montana was the centre of this hunting technique and has 245 buffalo jumps, while Alberta has 60, Saskatchewan 20, and North and South Dakota and Manitoba one each. All of the buffalo jumps face east and north, a reflection of the geomorphology, the prevailing winds, and the bison's acute sense of smell. The remains at buffalo jumps show a predominance of cows over bulls. Because female bison show a greater wariness and willingness to run, this may have made them more susceptible and preferable for driving.

Both the corral and the buffalo jump were dependent upon topographical features. The introduction of the horse enabled the Indian to hunt bison anywhere and anytime, and by 1750 all the tribes of the Canadian Plains were mounted. By 1780 bison hunting was commercialized, with Indians supplying hides and pemmican (dried bison meat mixed with fat and berries) to the fur trading posts in the north.

The bison was first eliminated from the American Plains. By 1850 meat and hide hunters were looking north to Canada to continue their livelihood. The northern bison herd is estimated to have contained 5-10 million animals, but it was decimated in less than three decades. After the hunters left, the bone pickers came. Bison bones commanded $6-10/ton. The bones were ground up and used in refining sugar. Horns were fashioned into buttons, combs and knife handles, and the hooves were turned into glue. The bone trade was over by the 1890's, and the herds were gone forever.

We may take some consolation from recent paleoclimatology studies. We now know that the average annual rainfall on the prairies decreased in the late 1800's. This produced a deterioration of the grasslands and a reduced capacity of the prairie to support large numbers of grazing animals. If the bison had not already been eliminated the grasslands would have been overstocked, and three-quarters of the bison population would have disappeared without interference from man.

A Matter of Rank

North Americans have frequently prided themselves on being a classless society where individuals are equal. From the standpoint of biology individuals are never equal, so they must compete. In the grassland community, competition is greatest for space, food and the right to reproduce. Certain patterns of social behavior have arisen among animal groups, ritualizing competition to minimize injury.

One pattern is the hierarchy system, in which individuals have a rank. The playful antics of coyote pups are early attempts to establish dominance, and serious fighting to establish rank occurs in coyotes as young as a month old. Once rank has been established it is unnecessary to repeat the competition for dominance. Confrontations between coyotes follow strict rules, and posture dictates social position. When a dominant coyote approaches another animal it walks with a stiff-legged gait, holding its tail at 45° to the vertical. With ears erect, it snarls and exposes its teeth. If the coyote being approached is of a lesser rank it flees, or else it assumes a submissive posture by lying on its back, flattening its ears against its head, whining and retracting its lip in a "submissive grin." A subordinate animal on occasion will approach one that is dominant. The animal approaches in a low crouch with its tail held low or tucked under its body. Usually it does this while whining and licking its face.

Fights only occur between dominant animals; otherwise violence would be maladaptive for the species. Dominant animals, which are the ones best suited to survive and pass on desirable traits, could be accidentally injured if they fought with a lesser animal. The ritualized behavior and habitual subordination of lesser animals maintains harmony and prevents unnecessary injury. Once established, the hierarchy is maintained by threats.

The social habits of coyotes varies, depending upon their food supply. Coyotes are solitary and interact very little, when small rodents are the principal food source. When larger prey is hunted the animals form loose packs, but these are not as permanent as the pack structures of wolves. In the grasslands, large mammals, such as deer, comprise less than 4% of the coyote's diet, so the animals are most often solitary, as they feed on smaller prey. In winter they rely on carrion for 25% of their diet, and several animals may gather at the carcass of a cow or deer. Then the animals become more social, and the hierarchy system becomes important.

Mule deer use olfactory signals as well as posturing in their hierarchy displays. Buck mule deer display by vigorously thrashing shrubs and small trees with their antlers. Following this, they urinate while rubbing together their tarsal glands, located on the inside of their hind legs. The odour from the secretions of the tarsal glands identifies the individual buck, and the smell of his urine reveals whether he is in poor or good physical condition. An animal in good condition burns fat whereas one in poor condition burns protein. Fat and protein have different metabolic byproducts which are excreted in the urine and detectable by smell to other animals.

Sparring is often included in the interactions of younger bucks. The animals carefully lock antlers then push and twist, attempting to knock the other one off balance. These short matches, lasting less than a minute, are frequently preceded and followed by "profiling." Profiling is an attempt to intimidate the other buck by displaying the neck and antler size. Serious fights are not frequent, and usually involve large bucks of similar size. In these matches, the animals rush and lock horns violently. These combats may result in injuries and are a last resort to establish dominance. Here the stakes are high, for the winner mates with the available females.

Mule deer often share their coulee habitat with the slightly smaller white-tailed deer, although the latter prefers the wooded areas adjacent to fields and along rivers. The white-tail does well in agricultural environments, and its population in the grasslands has increased since settlers arrived, but the mule deer population has declined. Both species of deer are browsers, and they gather in coulees to feed on chokecherry, saskatoon, buffaloberry, rose and snowberry shrubs. The deer are sometimes seen at dusk and dawn, but they are most active at night, as are many other coulee animals.

Silently, In The Night

There is nothing like a walk in a coulee at night to awaken your mind and send your blood rushing.

A thousand cautious eyes do scan, each shadow and
each form;
Aware are all, this night there treads a stranger to
this place.
The stranger moves as one who fears despite its size
and bulk,
And clammy skin that shines with sweat betrays an
inner stress.
With steps unsure and brain confused it slowly
wends it way,
Each sound is grasped with hungry ears, each smell
inhaled with zest.
Its eyes reach out like groping hands for shapes it
cannot see,

And in its head the circuits race to solve the
shadowed world.
In former times it roamed this land, and felt akin to
all,
But now it dwells where every step is marked by
glaring lights;
But for a time the stranger dared, as man returned
to night.

— Author

The creature most commonly associated with night is the owl. Two species of owls nest in the coulee habitat, the long-eared owl and the great horned owl. Both species have acute vision and sensitive hearing, essential qualities for a nocturnal hunter. Their wing surface is large, so very little wing movement is necessary. This reduces air turbulence and noise, so they fly silently. Also, their flight feathers are fringed at the front and rear, silencing their flight even more.

Small rodents are on the menu of both owls, but pinpointing a scurrying deer mouse on a moonless night takes some doing. The owls have large eardrums richly supplied with auditory nerves. A crow, twice the size of the long-eared owl, has 27,000 auditory nerves compared with the owl's 90,000. In both owls, the external auditory openings differ in size, and one is higher than the other. This asymmetry probably helps the owl to localize sounds. Owls have relatively wide heads so there is a delay between the time one ear receives a sound, and when the opposite ear receives it. This delay is critical to accurately locate the source of a sound, and it permits owls to capture prey in total darkness.

When I think of owls, I think of eyes. All birds have relatively large eyes, but the eyes of an owl can be larger than a man's. In owls, their visual fields overlap, so that their vision is binocular, and they perceive depth. They cannot move their eyes like humans so they swivel their heads through a 260° arc.

The owl's prey are not without their own defenses, and these include cryptic colouration, quick reflexes, wariness, sensitive hearing, fetid sprays and quills. In the ongoing

117

process of natural selection, predators and prey are constantly evolving new adaptations to thwart the other side. They are involved in an "arms race," with the predators developing new and better capture techniques, and the prey in turn developing strategies to foil these techniques. This competition has led to highly honed predators, and equally honed prey. A good example of this is found in the great horned owl, which, like most owls, has developed acute eyesight and hearing at the expense of its sense of smell. This has its advantages when skunks are on the menu. The great horned owl is the only significant enemy of the skunk.

The skunk is probably the best known of the grassland weasels. With its reputation, the skunk doesn't need speed or camouflage; in fact, its colour announces its presence, and it can afford to be peaceful and nonaggressive. That is not to say that skunks cannot be angered. When annoyed, they hiss and snarl and stamp their front feet. Sometimes they even do a momentary handstand on their forefeet, but they cannot spray from this position. The spray from a skunk is a thick, yellow, oily substance produced by glands located in the perianal region. The glands, which contain enough musk for 5-6 discharges, are surrounded by powerful muscles. When the muscles contract the musk is discharged through nozzle-like structures. Two fine streams are discharged and produce a spray of minute droplets that can reach a target up to six meters away in still air.

The skunk has long, straight claws. These are used for digging up the eggs of turtles and snakes, excavating the burrows of mice, and tearing apart logs for insects. It is the only member of the weasel family that dens up in the winter. A female and her four to six kits will overwinter together, and as many as twenty animals have been known to share the same winter den.

The skunk and the great horned owl are members of the same food chain, with the owl at the top, the skunk in the middle, and mice at the bottom. Food chains start with plants, and the energy stored in them is passed along through the ecosystem in a series of eating and being eaten.

Herbivores occupy the base of the food chain. In terms of quantity there are always more plants than herbivores and more herbivores than carnivores, so that food chains resemble pyramids. In the coulee, for example, a section of ravine might grow 1000 kilograms of vegetation which would feed 100 kilograms of mice, insects and ground squirrels. In turn, these will feed 10 kilograms of skunks and other weasels which would then feed 1 kilogram of coyotes and owls. At each step in the food chain the animals spend 90% of the energy they consume. They use this energy in reproduction, movement, digestion, growth and heat production. At any one step only 10% of the energy consumed is transferred to the next step. That is why there are fewer animals with each succeeding step in the chain, and why great horned owls and coyotes, which are at the top of the pyramid, always occur in relatively small numbers.

Wildlife at the top of the food chain is particularly susceptible to the detrimental effects of pesticides, which are widely used in forestry and agriculture to control harmful insects. Among pesticides, the chlorinated hydrocarbons arouse the greatest concern because, unlike others, their chemical structure resists breakdown and they remain in the environment long after their application.

Plant-eating animals such as mice and ground squirrels ingest pesticides that have been sprayed on plants, and if that does not kill them, the pesticide is stored in the animal's fatty tissue. The longer the animal eats food contaminated with chlorinated hydrocarbons, the higher will be the concentration of these chemicals in its fatty tissue. When the animal is eaten by a predator, the predator ingests chlorinated hydrocarbons in far higher concentrations than did the original plant-eater. The higher up an animal or bird sits on the food pyramid, the greater the concentration of pesticides it ingests, and the greater the likelihood that the pesticide will eventually poison the animal.

DDT, developed during World War II, was the first chlorinated hydrocarbon to be used, and its damaging effects on the ecosystem were felt within ten years of its introduction. Within twenty years, DDT had spread to every niche on the globe and was even detectable in the tissues of animals in

Antarctica which were far removed from any direct application of the chemical. Although the widespread use of DDT was discontinued after 1970, other chlorinated hydrocarbons continue to be used with as yet undetermined ecological effects. DDT was a warning of the potentially far-reaching and devastating effects these chemicals can have on the environment. Man is the final predator at the end of the food chain, and without care we may have to eat our own poisons.

Nightwings

Like the skunk, the bats of the grasslands escape winter by hibernating or migrating to warmer climates. There are a dozen species of bats in Canada, nine of which occur in the mixed grasslands. Half of the species of bats common to the grasslands live in colonies in abandoned buildings and caves; the others, which include the hoary bat, red bat and silver-haired bat are solitary, and spend the day in coulees, hanging among the foliage of trees or in hollow trunks. Bats share with us the characteristics common to all mammals. They are warm blooded, covered with hair, and their young are nourished through a placenta before birth, and with mammary glands after birth.

The wing of a bat is formed from a double layer of skin stretched between the hand and finger bones, and extending to the side of the body and the hind leg — unlike birds, whose wings are formed from bones analogous to our arm, wrist and hand, and are covered in feathers. Most bats also have an interfemoral membrane connecting the hind legs, and including the tail.

Bats have other features that distinguish them from birds. Bats have no nest, and their one or two naked young cling to their mother and accompany her on nightly hunting forays until they are old enough to stay behind. Birds catch insects with their mouths; bats catch them with their interfemoral membrane, which is folded forward and acts like a baseball mitt. Common to both bats and birds is the ability to digest food quickly and pass it rapidly through their intestines. This is highly beneficial, as it reduces the load that is carried in flight.

Tropical bats eat fruit, nectar, frogs, fish, birds, blood and other bats, but all Canadian bats are insect eaters, and all use sonar. The small eyes of bats are probably of little use in their night flights, and to compensate they have a sonar system for locating objects. As they fly they emit a series of supersonic clicks that bounce back from objects and are picked up again by the bats. This is called *echolocation*. Most of the sounds that humans hear have frequencies around several hundred cycles per second. A bat flying by sonar uses sounds between 50,000 and 200,000 cycles per second. Two advantages come from the use of such high frequencies for echolocation. The directional precision is much better with high frequencies. High frequencies permit detection of smaller objects. The little brown bat that echolocates in the 100,000 cycles per second range can detect an object 0.3 millimeters in size.

An inherent disadvantage with high frequency echolocation is its limited range, which means that the bat must be close to its prey to detect it. This works to the advantage of certain moths who can hear the bat before the bat can detect them. When a moth hears a bat it abandons its usual cruising flight, and goes into sharp dives or erratic loops, or it flies at top speed directly away from the source of the supersonic sounds. The moths can detect the high frequencies with ears located on the sides of their thorax. Each ear is externally visible as a small cavity, and within the cavity is a transparent eardrum. In the "arms race" between bats and moths, the bats have evolved speed and echolocation, and the moths have developed evasive flight and specialized ears.

Bats live in a different sensory world from ours, a world we are only beginning to understand. With the aid of sophisticated auditory equipment we can now listen to the calls of bats, and newly developed electronic image intensifiers allow us to see and photograph bats at night in total darkness. In time, technology will help us to understand the bat, and change its poor image with the public, which associates bats with death, disease and Dracula. Throughout the book, I have dealt with both the "beauties" and the "beasts" of the animal world; it is my hope that we can all recognize the worth of both.

Geese Going Days

The Indians kept track of time by observing the cycles of nature, and the passage from one season to the next was often marked by the movements of animals. Cackling geese wedging across an October sky marked the return of autumn, the season when coulees ignite with colour.

The shimmering golds of autumn aspens that cloak the bottoms of coulees, and the rich ambers of cottonwoods that skirt the banks of rivers result from pigments that were always present but were masked during the growing season. Within every leaf there is a blend of inherently colourful substances. Daylength, temperature, and rainfall determines which of these colourful substances will dominate in the different seasons. In spring and summer, the most abundant substance is the pigment chlorophyll which imparts the green colour to foliage. Chlorophyll is vital to plants; it captures the sun's energy and uses it to manufacture simple sugars that are the basis of the plant's nourishment. Sunlight is also required for the synthesis of chlorophyll itself. During the growing season when days are long and sunlight plentiful, chlorophyll is synthesized continually so that the supply remains high and the leaves stay green. In autumn, the diminishing hours of daylight and the cool temperatures slow the rate at which chlorophyll is synthesized. With the total amount of chlorophyll dwindling, its masking effect fades and other colourful substances begin to show through.

One group of substances is the *carotenoids*, yellow pigments that confer the Midas touch to aspens, cottonwoods, alders, birches and Manitoba maples. Carotenoids, unlike chlorophyll, do not need sunlight for their synthesis and they are unaffected by the shortening days of autumn.

The reds and purples of coulee dogwoods and other shrubs result from the presence of another group of pigments called *anthocyanins*. These pigments are not present throughout the growing season as are the carotenoids and they develop only in late summer as a result of a change in the metabolic breakdown of sugar. Anthocyanins also colour many of the coulee fruits such as pincherries, strawberries, raspberries, saskatoons and rose hips.

In late summer, a corky layer of cells forms at the base of each leaf stem. These cells prevent the passage of minerals, water and other nutrients from the roots to the leaves and vice versa. This layer gradually weakens the attachment of the leaf, and eventually the wind snaps the leaf free.

Leaves are lost in autumn because it is the most economical way for a tree to survive the winter. Leaves continually lose water through surface pores which are open to absorb carbon dioxide for the manufacture of sugar. The manufacture of sugar ceases when the temperature becomes cold, and if the tree were to retain its leaves it would continue to lose moisture without any benefit. Moreover, once the ground is frozen the tree cannot extract water from the soil to replenish its losses. If leaves were retained during winter they would become heavy with a burden of ice and snow and would invariably break off, taking with them important nutrients essential for the welfare of the tree. Deciduous trees drain 95% of the minerals and other nutrients from the leaves before they are cast off, and store these materials for the next growing season.

The trees of the coulee are able to survive in the grasslands because they are sheltered from dessicating winds and receive moisture from runoff.

The yellow warbler has the greatest range of any wood warbler. It nests from the Arctic to Mexico and from the Atlantic to the Pacific. It favours the edges of waterways bordered by willows and alders, and thickets grown up with raspberry, chokecherry and rose.

Twin fawns are the rule for white-tailed deer. Although newborn fawns can get to their feet within minutes of birth, they remain feeble for several weeks. During this period they lay hidden for hours at a time and the doe returns at intervals to suckle.

Young red foxes lick each other's face in recognition.

The bull snake is the longest snake in the grasslands, attaining lengths of two meters. Despite its size it has a gentle disposition and it can be handled readily.

The specialized skin that covers the growing antlers of the white-tailed deer is called "velvet." The velvet is sensitive to pain and touch and this helps to prevent injury to the fast growing antlers.

The feathered ear tufts of the long eared owl are ornamental and not linked with hearing.

The deeply furrowed bark of the Manitoba maple, or box elder, darkens with age. It is a fast growing, medium sized tree (12-16 meters high, 0.3-0.6 meters in diameter) found in coulees in Saskatchewan and Manitoba. Its hardiness has made it popular on the prairies for shelter belts.

Each seed of the goatsbeard has its own parachute of fine silk. When the wind finally plucks the seeds free they can be carried great distances.

Young skunks are born in early May, usually 5 or 6 to a litter. At birth they are blind, and are confined to their natal den, but by late June they accompany their mother, following in single file.

Chemical receptors are abundant on the antennae, legs, and mouth parts of the red admiral butterfly, and are important in communication. Odour signals, called pheromones, are now known to determine many aspects of insect behaviour.

The Bohemian waxwing is a winter visitor to the mixed grasslands. Late in autumn large flocks appear in cities and towns to feast on the fruits of ornamental trees and shrubs. They are particularly fond of the red berries of the mountain ash.

Moist coulees are the habitat of false solomon's seal. In late summer the plant is topped with crimson berries.

Water and Wings

Photographing in the wetlands takes a special brand of dedication. In my early years I took no special measures, and simply accepted that to get wet and cold was the price one paid to photograph in such areas. Eventually, I progressed to chest waders. These were fine for a while until I got mired several times in the bottoms of sloughs, and had to waddle to shore with more water inside the boots than out. I now stalk the wetlands in a black rubber wetsuit. I love to explode from the cattails that surround a slough beside the Trans Canada Highway, dressed in clinging black neoprene and sporting a green mosquito head net, and watch the expression on the faces of motorists as they pass. Usually I find them pulled over for a rest a few miles up the road.

The general undulating topography of the mixed grass prairie results in millions of natural depressions. When these depressions fill with water they are called sloughs. Sloughs are essential to the vitality of the mixed grasslands and they are the principal wetlands habitat.

Sloughs differ from small lakes and ponds. They have no streams draining into or out of them, and receive their water as runoff in spring. Many sloughs dry up in summer, and in the most arid regions of the grasslands a third of them disappear by mid-July. The transient nature of sloughs does not seem to discourage the use of them by wildlife. Over 50% of all ducks in North America, and 80% of all redheads, canvasbacks, pintails and mallards, start life on a prairie slough. Sloughs attract blackbirds, grebes, herons, bitterns, avocets and willets, and they are essential in the reproductive cycle of grassland frogs and toads. They also serve as feeding and resting areas for shorebirds on their spring and fall migrations.

Sloughs are frequently shallow and transient, yet they are much more productive of wildlife than the more numerous permanent lakes found farther north in the boreal forest and tundra ecosystems. Sloughs are rich in nutrients washed in by surface drainage. These nutrients are concentrated by evaporation, and the resulting high fertility encourages the proliferation of invertebrates, algae, duckweeds, and pondweeds which nourish wildlife. The lakes of the boreal forest and tundra are acidic and consequently have lower fertility and produce only a tenth as many invertebrates per volume of water as do sloughs. Moreover, ducks like to be spaced so that many tiny sloughs are better than a single large lake.

One characteristic of sloughs is that they differ. Some sloughs are ringed with bulrushes and cattails, others have a perimeter of willows and aspens; some have a "bath tub" ring of white alkali salt with an outer ring of snowberry and rose shrubs, and still others have seemingly no vegetation at all surrounding them. There are large sloughs and tiny sloughs, although the average size is half a hectare, and sloughs can be deep or shallow, but those with less than 40 centimeters are generally dry by midsummer.

All sloughs are transitional and are forever in a process of change. The change may be rapid or exceedingly slow depending upon a number of factors. Ultimately, every slough is destined to disappear, though possibly not for thousands of years. Each will eventually be filled in with sediment and converted to grasslands, the climax habitat of the mixed grass prairie. Following a typical slough through a succession of stages, it is possible to understand why sloughs often look so different from one another, and to see how the plants and animals change with time.

The Evolution of a Slough

The first stage in the life of a slough is the *pioneer stage,* characterized by a bottom which is barren of plant life. This stage was common to all sloughs that existed at the end of the Ice Age, immediately after the glaciers retreated from the prairie region. The earliest colonizers of a slough are plankton (microscopic plants and animals) that are carried on the legs of birds, which inadvertently seed the slough. The rich minerals, warm water temperatures and sunshine lead to a proliferation of the plankton. These minute organisms grow, reproduce, die and settle to the bottom of the slough, adding to its fertility and building up a layer of organic muck.

Waterfowl use the slough as loafing and preening areas. During grooming, seeds of pondweeds and filamentous algae are knocked loose from the bird's feathers and legs, and root in the oozy material on the bottom of the slough. The roots of these submerged aquatic plants bind the ooze together, and when they die they add to the material accumulating on the bottom. At this stage, snails, mayflies, scarlet water mites and numerous other invertebrates appear, transported by animals, birds and the wind.

The continued addition of organic matter reduces the depth of the slough. In the next stage, the *floating aquatic stage*, floating plants such as watercrowfoot and bladderwort take root. Their floating leaves shelter a host of new residents, including frogs, diving beetles and dozens of other insects. The leaves spread out over the surface of the slough in their competition for light, so that very little light reaches the depths of the slough, and the submerged pondweeds are unable to continue photosynthesis. They die and add their tissues to the bottom ooze. The fertile muck now supports a rich bottom fauna of dragonfly nymphs, worms and leeches. Once, and only once, did I sit in a blind with my bare feet planted in the bottom ooze of a slough. Unknown to me, within that ooze lurked formidable jaws, and I suffered for a week with swollen, bitten feet that itched incessantly.

The floating aquatic plants need the protection and buoyancy of water, and they disappear first from the perimeter of the slough. Once the shallow edges of the slough fill with sediment there is not enough water to support their soft stems. The emergent plants move in and fill the void. These plants have strong, flexible stems, and narrow leaves that bend easily before the wind and water. The emergents partition the shallow water; bulrushes, cattails and sedges grow farthest from shore, and closer in grow the smartweeds, arrowheads, rushes and spikerushes. In the evolution of a slough, this is called the *emergent stage*. Ducks, herons and flamboyant yellow-headed and red-winged blackbirds become its conspicuous residents, feeding and nesting among the forest of emergent stems.

If the slough is deep and survives for years, willows will form a partial or complete margin about the slough. The trees break the wind and lessen the losses to evaporation. In winter the snow piles up around the trees, and greater amounts of meltwater rejuvenate the slough the following spring.

Meanwhile, in the center of the slough, the burden of floating aquatic vegetation starts to take its toll. The water becomes depleted of oxygen from the decay of accumulating bottom debris. In summer elevated water temperatures aggravate the oxygen shortage by accelerating the decay. At this stage only animals with low oxygen requirements find the bottom habitable. The march of the emergent plants continues, their dense fibrous roots securing their position. A time comes when much of the old open water area is covered by bulrushes with an outer rim of cattails and sedges.

The evolution of a slough is not always the steady forward progression outlined so far. Topography, climate, erosion and the effects of wildlife and livestock combine to dictate its evolution, which can be fast or slow, steady or stuttered, backwards or forwards. A slough may move rapidly forward through several stages and then became stalled in a stage for centuries, and finally revert back to an earlier stage. In wet years the submerged and floating aquatic plants flourish, whereas in years of drought the emergent cattails and bulrushes will dominate.

As the bottom rises, the slough dries up in summer and becomes a temporary slough, as are a third of the sloughs in the mixed grasslands. Then, only animals such as insects, that can withstand drying in summer and freezing in winter, persist. The surrounding grasses start to reclaim the old area of the slough when it dries up.

The water of sloughs is very salty because sloughs are fed by heavily mineralized runoff water, and also because they are subject to high evaporation rates which concentrate the salts. When the sloughs disappear the salts remain behind. The principal salts are calcium sulphate (gypsum), magnesium sulphate (Epsom salts), and sodium sulphate (Glaubers salts). Most grasses and other plants cannot survive in salty soil because the soil draws water out of the plant, and the plant withers and dies. One group of plants, called *halophytes*, are able to increase the salt concentration within their own tissues beyond the concentration of salts in the soil, and therefore draw in water and survive. This stage in the evolution of a slough, the one dominated by halophytes, can be termed the *saline grassland stage*.

The salt concentration is highest in the center of the old slough where the water disappeared last, and decreases proportionately away from this point. Since halophytes vary in their ability to tolerate salts, concentric bands of vegetation form, with the most salt-tolerant species in the center, and the least tolerant species at the periphery, where they merge with the usual mixed grasses of the region. At the center of a saline grassland are the halophytes samphire and arrowgrass; next are alkali grass and salt grass; and on the outside are foxtail barley and northern and western wheatgrass.

As the saline grassland ages, generations of halophytes die and build up the soil, and the scanty annual rainfall slowly leaches out the salts. Eventually the halophytes are replaced by the usual spectrum of mixed grasses, and the *climax stage* is reached.

Insects of the Slough

At every stage in the life of a slough the most abundant animals are insects. Insects are the most successful terrestrial animals on earth, and 75% of all animals are insects. The slough habitat has a full complement of insect inhabitants. Some are secretive and submerged, others are colourful and conspicuous.

Dozens of species of mosquitoes have been identified from the sloughs of the grasslands. Because of their roles as vectors in many human diseases, mosquitoes have been studied extensively and their natural history is well known.

Mosquitoes will utilize almost any small body of water as a breeding site, from sloughs and ditches to stagnant water in an old bucket. Only females are bloodsucking, while male mosquitoes of all species feed solely on nectar and plant juices. Female mosquitoes will also feed on plant juices for energy, but they need blood to produce eggs. Most species of mosquito feed on a specific host, either reptiles, birds or mammals. But it is hard to believe that mosquitoes are interested in anything other than humans when you stroll around a slough on a warm summer evening. Different species feed at different times of the day, so it is possible to be punctured in the morning by one species, riddled at noon by others, feasted upon at dusk by yet another, and attacked at night by several more. Mosquitoes are attracted to us by our perspiration and the carbon dioxide we exhale, and women become more enticing during ovulation when they have higher blood estrogen levels.

Another common and conspicuous inhabitant of the slough is the dragonfly. Coloured in greens, golds and reds, dragonflies are fast flying, predatory insects that feed on other insects, particularly mosquitoes and midges. They catch their prey on the wing, and for this they need good vision. Dragonflies have large, compound eyes. Compound eyes cannot be closed, moved, or focused, but they are ideal for detecting movement, and they see in many directions at the same time. Compound eyes are found in many insects but they are most highly developed in the dragonfly. A compound eye is composed of thousands of long cylindrical units, called *omatidia*, each of which receives light and produces an image. The number of omatidia is a reflection of the behavior of the insect. Honey bees have 4000 omatidia and swallowtail butterflies have 17000. Both insects feed on flowers which are stationary and are generally conspicuously coloured. The predaceous dragonfly has 28000 omatidia, as it feeds on prey that is small and fast-flying.

There are two insects in the slough that cannot seem to make up their minds whether to live in air, or live in water. The water strider and the whirligig beetle live in the interface between air and water. In any body of water, the molecules of the liquid are attracted to each other. At the surface the water molecules are not attracted evenly from all sides, so the surface responds like a stretched membrane, and thus it can support objects with a greater density than water itself. It allows water striders and whirligig beetles to stand and move on it.

The whirligig beetle is a round, black beetle that can dive or fly, but it usually plows through the surface film half in and half out of the water. It has divided compound eyes, with the lower half recording events below the surface and the upper half recording above the surface. The whirligig beetle rests its antennae on the surface of the water to detect ripples reflected back from objects in its course, and so avoids collisions. Their swift responses allow dozens of whirligigs to move about the same patch of slough without colliding.

The water strider lives on top of the surface film and skates along the surface, rowing with its middle pair of long legs. When an insect from below comes to the surface for air the strider stabs the insect with its sharp mouth parts and injects digestive saliva. It then sucks out the liquefied contents, and the empty shell of the victim drifts to the bottom of the slough.

Water striders will hide when you approach the edge of the slough, but they are much more sensitive to vibrations on the water surface. Striders detect these vibrations with sensors in their legs. They use ripples in the water to communicate ownership, courtship and aggression. When a male strider is ready to mate and he has found a suitable mating site, such as floating vegetation, a feather or a piece of wood, he taps on the water and sends out a message with a specific frequency of ripples to attract a female. When the female approaches, the male switches to a different pattern of ripples with a faster frequency, and when the female is within a few centimeters of the male she also sends out courtship ripples. The male defends his mating site and the female from other male striders by producing aggressive signals, which again are a specific pattern of ripples. Each species of strider has its own unique repertoire of ripple patterns.

Songsters of the Night

Courtship brings out the talkativeness in all animals, and some of the most loquacious in their pursuit of carnal gratification are the frogs and toads, who never say a word until it is time to mate.

In the evolutionary succession, amphibians (frogs, toads, and salamanders) followed fish. They developed a skeleton to support them away from the buoyancy of water, and lungs to breathe air. But amphibians have never become completely emancipated from water, as did the later evolving reptiles, birds and mammals. The amphibians' dependence on water is most apparent when you consider their reproduction. Frogs and toads court, mate and lay their eggs in water, and they spend the early phase of their lives as aquatic tadpoles. Three species of frogs are found in the mixed grasslands: the wood frog, the boreal chorus frog and the leopard frog.

The boreal chorus frog is the smallest of the three frogs, with a maximum length of 3.5 centimeters. It breeds earlier than other frogs; mating begins as soon as the snow has melted and temperatures rise in mid-April. The boreal chorus frog has a surprisingly loud and penetrating call for its size, and its call can be mimicked quite well by running a fingernail along the teeth of a small comb. The male chorus frogs gather around the periphery of a slough and each frog calls from its own small territory. The songs of all frogs are specific for each species, and the songs differ in frequency, duration, and the number of notes. The hearing of female frogs is most sensitive to the frequencies of its own species, so that they essentially hear only the calls of their own males, although four or five species of amphibians may be calling in the same slough on the same night.

Frogs are perfunctory lovers. They have dispensed with elaborate courtship displays and foreplay in favour of the croak and grab approach. A calling male does not discriminate, and will grab any frog that comes into his territory, including other males and frogs of another species. In cases of misidentification the 'grabbee' immediately notifies the 'grabber' with a grunt, and the grabbee is released. In the sexual embrace of frogs, called *amplexus*, the male jumps on the back of the female, and clasps her behind the forelegs or in front of the hindlegs. Many male frogs have spiny nuptial pads on their forefeet to assist in holding the female during amplexus. When the eggs are laid, the male simply floods them with sperm. The simultaneous release of sperm and eggs seems to be synchronized by subtle body movements of the female.

The eggs of amphibians have no shells to prevent them from drying out, so they are laid in water with only a coating of jelly for protection. The wood frog, which is well adapted to northern climates, and ranges the farthest north of any frog in North America, attaches its eggs to plant stems a few centimeters below the surface of the water to avoid the severe temperature fluctuations of surface water. In northern populations, its eggs are larger and darker, to increase the amount of solar energy absorbed, which in turn determines the rate of embryonic development.

The transformation from aquatic, gill breathing, vegetarian tadpoles to terrestrial, lung breathing, carnivorous adult frogs is the most remarkable phenomenon in the lives of frogs. Under the control of the thyroid gland, the round mouth of the tadpole widens and develops a tongue, and its teeth are shed. Nostrils and lungs appear and the external gills shrink. Limbs gradually lengthen, and the tail is absorbed. The transformation is orderly and exquisitely timed. The swimming tail does not shrink before the jumping legs have grown, and the nostrils and lungs appear before the gills are resorbed.

The Muskrat

At the start of every season I make a list of the animals that I want to photograph, and every season the list includes the muskrat. I lie in bed at night visualizing the ultimate muskrat photograph. I plan ways of getting inside their lodges, and following them underwater. Many of my best photographs started with pre-visualization, and I was to follow my ideas through to success. However, the definitive photograph of the muskrat still eludes me, and I expect it will continue to appear on my seasonal photo lists for some time to come.

The muskrat, possibly the most widely distributed mammal in North America, is a large rodent found in sloughs throughout the mixed grassland. A suitable slough must have a depth of one to two meters so that the water does not freeze to the bottom in winter. Also, there should be good growths of bulrushes, sedges, pondweeds and especially cattails, which are the muskrat's favorite food.

Muskrats live in lodges set in the water. In the absence of suitable building materials, muskrats will dig a burrow into the banks of the slough. The muskrat builds its lodge by first heaping mud and plant material into a pile, then digging an entrance into the mound from underwater and chewing out an interior chamber. The typical lodge is usually a meter high and a meter in diameter. When the slough first freezes in winter, the muskrat chews holes through the ice, up to 100 meters from its lodge, and stuffs vegetation and mud through the hole and fashions it into a protective dome. These miniature lodges or 'push-ups' are used for resting and feeding, and usually hold only one muskrat.

The muskrat is well adapted to its aquatic environment, and by three weeks of age it is a capable diver and swimmer. They can stay submerged for as long as fifteen minutes, an essential adaptation when foraging for food under the ice in winter. Muskrats share several characteristics common to all diving mammals. Their muscles contain high levels of hemoglobin which stores oxygen and surrenders it slowly during a dive. While the muskrat is submerged, blood is shunted away from the muscles, skin and gut, and the oxygen which is carried in the blood is saved for the heart and brain. Muskrats swim with alternating strokes of their hindlegs, while their forelegs are tucked against the chest, and their scaly flat tail is used as both a rudder and a propeller. The feet of the muskrat are unlike the webbed feet of the beaver; the muskrat has toes that are fingered with stiff hairs.

Throughout the years, and especially in winter when the

slough is frozen, the muskrat must chew underwater without choking. The animal's lips and cheeks close behind its incisors and no water enters the mouth. Like all rodents, the muskrat has two pairs of chisel-like incisor teeth that grow throughout its life. These have hard enamel on the front surface and softer material on the inside so that they acquire a beveled tip as a result of uneven wear. A broken tooth can be a tragic event as the opposite tooth will continue to grow unchecked, and may eventually obstruct the animal's bite.

Dabblers and Divers

If you watch the ducks on a slough you will notice that ducks are divided into two main groups, divers and dabblers, according to their feeding habits. Divers swim in the middle of the slough and dive underwater for food, while dabblers paddle along the edges and feed off the surface, or else they tip their bottoms up to reach food just below the surface.

The prairie dabblers include the familiar mallard, the pintail and shoveller, the three species of teal, the gadwall and the widgeon. All of the dabblers have their legs positioned in the center of their body, and when they fly they jump straight off the water. On land they walk with a characteristic waddle. The dabblers frequently nest up to a mile away from the slough. They nest in uncropped grasses or in clumps of snowberry, rose and silverberry bushes, and along fence rows. The shallow periphery of the slough, where dabblers feed, is partitioned to avoid competition. For example, pintails feed closest to shore on bottom vegetation, while gadwall and widgeon feed just offshore on submerged vegetation; the gadwall feeds on surface food and the widgeon on food just below the surface.

The canvasback, redhead and scaup are prairie divers. The diving ducks have their legs positioned near the rear of the body where the leg muscles interfere least with streamlining. It is also best for propulsion and steering. The divers run along the surface of the water before taking flight. On land their walk is clumsy, and they prefer to rest on the water rather than on shore with the dabblers. The divers nest in the slough, and the nest is typically a bulky structure of plant materials well-hidden in the cattails or bulrushes. Diving ducks also partition their section of the habitat for feeding. Canvasbacks and redheads feed on bottom invertebrates, and scaup feed in the deepest water on swimming invertebrates.

Ducks live in water, but their skin never gets wet. They keep their plumage waterproof by applying oil to their feathers, which repels the water. When grooming, the bird frequently rubs its head and bill at the base of its back. This is the location of the preen gland, which produces an oily, waxy secretion that is fastidiously spread over all of the plumage. The preen gland is largest in aquatic birds, and ducks may preen as often as seventeen times a day. When young ducklings hatch, the adults preen even more, as frequently as several times an hour. A possible explanation is that oil is spread from the adult's plumage to the downy young, although young ducklings instinctively perform preening movements when only a day old. The oily secretions not only keep a duck's feathers healthy and waterproof, but also keep its legs and bill from drying out. If a duck stops preening, the feathers, legs and bill quickly deteriorate.

All ducks are strong fliers, but a body designed for strong flight cannot be optimally shaped for food diving; therefore all of the diving ducks have had to compromise their aquatic proficiency. Among the water birds of the slough, the grebes occupy the opposite end of the spectrum. Grebes are relatively weak fliers, but proficient divers.

Prairie Grebes

Five species of grebes nest in the sloughs of the mixed grasslands, and although they are frequently mistaken for ducks, they are altogether different. Whereas a duck's bill is blunt and flattened for sifting through mud and plant material, the grebe's bill is slim and pointed for feeding on aquatic beetles, larvae, worms and crustaceans. Grebes are superlative divers, and their legs are positioned farther to the rear than any of the diving ducks. Their feathers trap less air, their bones are more solid, and their air sacs smaller — features that make grebes less buoyant than ducks, and therefore better divers. Grebes are most secure in the water, and when alarmed they will dive rather than fly.

If I were an egg, the first place I would choose to be laid would be in a duck's nest, and the last place would be in a grebe's nest. In a duck's nest I would be dry and nestled in fluffy, warm down. In a grebe's nest I would be wet, jostled and dirty. Grebes build floating nests of decaying vegetation and the eggs often sit in water. On windy days, the water in sloughs can be whipped into waves that may capsize the nest and wash out the eggs. Grebe's eggs are whitish when they are first laid, but they soon become stained brown from the fermenting vegetation. The single consolation in my life as a grebe's egg would be that when I hatch I could ride on my parents' backs, and clamber aboard anytime for a rest or for warmth.

Sloughs concentrate salts, so that the water, the vegetation and invertebrate life are high in salt content. It is therefore essential that grebes and other water birds be able to excrete large amounts of salt, or they will face dehydration. For this purpose they have specialized salt glands located above the inside corner of each eye to eliminate excess salt from their blood. The salt glands become even more important for grebes along their wintering grounds on the Atlantic and Pacific coasts, where they must eat marine invertebrates and drink salt water.

The eared, horned and pied-billed grebes are the three smallest of the prairie grebes, and all have extensive ranges that overlap in the Canadian mixed grasslands. When animals overlap in their distributions they can only coexist if they differ either in their habitat or in the foods that they eat. Different food preferences between the different species of prairie ducks allow them to successfully partition the slough and lessen the competition between them, and it would be reasonable to assume that a similar diet strategy could work for grebes. In fact, the three grebes do display different preferences for fish as well as subtle differences in feeding technique on their marine wintering grounds and on lakes in British Columbia. But there are no fish in prairie sloughs and studies have shown that the three species of grebes must feed on the same insect and invertebrate life when they nest in the grasslands. Therefore the grebes can coexist only by selecting different slough habitats.

The eared grebe nests in groups and selects lakes and large open sloughs for its colonies which may contain over a hundred nesting pairs. The pied-billed grebe and the horned grebe are solitary nesters and they nest on small sloughs. Usually each slough has only one nesting pair. Although the horned and pied-billed grebes prefer the same size slough they prefer different amounts of emergent vegetation to be present. Pied-billed grebes prefer heavily vegetated sloughs while horned grebes need very little vegetation and will sometimes nest in completely open water on sloughs that are seasonally tilled and have no emergent vegetation. However, in such open water the nests are frequently swamped by waves and lost.

Sun Seekers

Every autumn thousands of tiny yellow warblers, each weighing only a few grams, fly more than 3000 kilometers to their wintering grounds in Mexico. For a human to achieve an equivalent feat would require travelling 24,000,000 kilometers, six times the distance from the earth to the moon.

Such prodigious movements are common among migratory birds that summer in the temperate and higher latitudes of North America. Of the nearly two hundred species of birds nesting in the mixed grasslands, at least 85% migrate to more clement climes to avoid the rigours of winter. But migration carries risks. Predators, human hunters, disorientation, starvation, exhaustion, and collision with man-made structures exact a heavy toll. Some radio and television towers rise hundreds of meters into the air and are supported by guy wires that extend out from the tower half a kilometer. In the United States, over ten thousand migrants died in collisions with one such tower in the course of two consecutive nights. To offset the many risks of migration, birds must accumulate adequate fuel in the form of fat, precisely time the moment of their departure, select a migration route, and finally, successfully navigate a lengthy course over largely unfamiliar terrain.

The Arctic nesting shorebirds: sandpipers, plovers, dowitchers, and phalaropes, are the first migrants to revisit the slough in autumn on their journey south. These birds may start to migrate as early as August, long before inclement weather or a shortage of food has compelled them to leave. An innate annual rhythm regulates many aspects of bird behaviour and in this particular instance, their urge to migrate. In northern birds, this innate rhythm is further modified and finely tuned by certain cues from the environment, especially daylength. In the Arctic, the decreasing hours of daylight associated with late summer signal the imminent approach of winter, and birds become restless and are thus stimulated to leave. All migrating birds exhibit this restlessness that drives them to migrate, and the timing of this restlessness has evolved over millenia to benefit the species.

Shorebirds, as well as ducks, geese, gulls, terns and grebes, migrate at night and during the day, but many other species are more selective. Most small passerine birds, such as, warblers, vireos, thrushes, sparrows and flycatchers, that normally reside in thickly vegetated protective habitats migrate only at night under the cover of darkness. Nocturnal migration allows them to avoid their usual diurnal predators, and also enables them to use the daylight hours to feed when they normally would. Daytime migrants include hawks, eagles and vultures. These birds use thermal updraughts that occur during the day to assist them in flight, and presumably this reduces the energy cost of migration.

Many migrants travel to the southern United States, Mexico or Central America, and some fly as far as the tropics of South America. Although most birds break their journey into sections with stopovers for feeding and resting, some geese have been known to fly sixty hours nonstop, covering 2500 kilometers.

Relatively few migrants travel beyond the tropics of South America, but there are two birds in the grasslands that

do. Both the nighthawk and Swainson's hawk frequently overwinter in Argentina, an annual round trip of 25,000 kilometers. For the Swainson's hawk, this is the longest migration flight of any member of the hawk family in North America.

Birds live in an expanded sensory world compared to that of humans. Some birds can detect polarized and ultra-violet light, and can measure the angle of the sun. Some can detect minor changes in barometric pressure in advance of a storm. Others can hear the low frequency sounds emanating from pounding surf from hundreds of feet in the air or detect the invisible force of the earth's magnetic field. Migrating birds use some or all of these cues to aid them in navigation.

Since birds have such good eyesight, it is reasonable to suppose that they use vision to navigate, and that they might use celestial cues such as the sun, moon and stars to guide them. In an intriguing series of experiments it was shown that birds do indeed use the sun to orient themselves. Furthermore, they can adjust for the changing angle of the sun with the seasons and to do so they must possess an internal clock that accurately senses the passage of time. But many birds migrate at night when the sun is invisible. To prove that birds can use stars to navigate, cages were built in which the roofs contained rotating star maps. Consistently, the birds detected changes in positions of the stars and adjusted their direction appropriately.

It has been known for a long time that birds recognize landmarks such as coastlines, mountain ranges and large waterways and follow them in migration. More recent, however, is the discovery that a number of birds are affected by the magnetic field of the earth. These birds may have permanent magnets within their heads that work like a compass as a navigational aid. Accumulations of magnetic material have been found in the neck muscles and heads of homing pigeons, white-crowned sparrows, tree swallows, western grebes and pintail ducks. This discovery is an exciting one, but in the final analysis it will undoubtedly prove to be only one of many aids that are used by birds to navigate.

The dance of the marbled godwit is repeated frequently during courtship. The female assumes the posture of the bird on the left when she has accepted her mate and wishes to solicit copulation.

The raccoon forages along the edge of sloughs; it is especially adept at flicking frogs and crustaceans out of the water with its paws, to add to its staple diet of nuts, seeds, fruit, insects and eggs.

146

The yellow-headed blackbird will only nest in vegetation where there is standing water. It displaces the red-winged blackbird, and relegates it to the periphery of the slough.

The male red-winged blackbird sings from old cattails to advertise its territory. It is very aggressive in defending its section of marsh, and the bird will attack crows, magpies and even hawks.

The creeping rootstalks of the cattail were dried by the Plains Indians and ground into a nutritious flour. They also used the leaves for weaving mats and baskets.

The Canada goose migrates both by day and by night. Its 1½ meter wingspan drives the bird at speeds of 60-100 kph.

The long filamentous plumes on the lower neck of the great blue heron are part of its nuptial plumage.

Although feathers are resilient and tough, the tips gradually wear away or break. All birds moult and replace all of their feathers at least once a year, most commonly after the breeding season.

Unlike most birds, the Canada goose family does not break up at the end of the breeding season. The parents and young establish strong family bonds and migrate together in autumn.

The speed of the peregrine falcon in its power dive has been estimated at 150-250 kph.

The eared grebe frequently nests in dense colonies sometimes containing over a hundred nests. Generally, 3-4 eggs are laid in late May and the male and female share the 21 day incubation period.

The blue-winged teal, unlike most dabbling ducks, rarely tips with its feet and tail in the air, but skims the seeds of pondweeds, grasses, and smartweeds from the surface, or reaches underwater with its head and neck.

In the phalaropes, the role of the sexes is reversed; females are larger and more brightly coloured, and they initiate courtship. The drably-feathered male Wilson's phalarope pictured will build a nest, incubate the eggs and rear the young.

In this, the final stage of a saline slough, a crust of sodium sulphate, calcium sulphate and magnesium sulphate rims the open water. The visible salts are a minor fraction of the total in the soil.

The horned grebe, like all grebes, has soft, thick lustrous plumage. Its breast feathers were once used in the millinery trade to decorate women's hats.

In Canada, the white pelican is a threatened species, and the population appears to be declining. Its breeding requirements are quite specific. The site must be a remote island, largely free of tree cover, inaccessible to mammalian predators, and close to a good food supply. The major factor in the pelican's recent decline appears to be human disturbance at nesting colonies, leading to abandonment.

The avocet feeds in shallow water on beetles, flies, dragonfly nymphs and crustaceans. It sweeps its partly opened bill from side to side underwater and stirs up aquatic life from the bottom.

Epilogue

As early as 1832 the American artist, George Catlin, expressed the need to preserve the beauty and splendor of the grasslands in a national park, and this was forty years before there were national parks of any kind in the world. In June 1981 an agreement was signed to establish a Grasslands National Park, designed to preserve and protect the integrity of the mixed grassland ecosystem of southwest Saskatchewan. We must be reserved in our enthusiasm, however, for national parks are always subject to the whims of politicians. Previously, we had three grassland national parks in Canada, and all of them came and went. In 1922 three tiny parks, Nemiskam, Wawaskesy and Menissawok, were set up in southern Alberta and Saskatchewan. These parks were established to halt the precipitous decline of the pronghorn population. By 1947 all three parks had been abolished. Pronghorn numbers had risen favourably and the parks were no longer considered necessary. The finalization of the present Grasslands National Park is still years away, and continued surveillance will be crucial to ensure a favourable outcome. To leave the park in the unfettered hands of political pundits would be foolish and naive. We again have a Grasslands National Park; this time let us keep it.

Preserving the grassland ecosystem entails more than setting aside a national park. We must alter how we view the environment, and what we see as our role. Today magpies and crows are still shot as vermin; coyotes and bobcats are hunted and trapped for fashion; and snakes of all kinds are beaten with sticks and labelled as worthless. Prairie dogs, considered to be pests, are poisoned, and children still flood the burrows of ground squirrels and strangle the animals when they try to escape. Every year, more sloughs succumb to the plow. The current formula for determining grain quotas encourages farmers to cultivate marginal lands such as sloughs, even when the projected yield is meagre.

The commonality still believe that air, water, vegetation, and wildlife are economic assets to be developed and turned into profit for the self-aggrandizement of man. Somehow we think that we have an intrinsic right to these assets. Although man controls the earth, he does not own the earth. Ethically we must respect all forms of life, and we have a responsibility to pass a rich natural heritage to future generations.

In the introduction of the book I outlined my intention to introduce the reader to the beauty and complexity of Canada's mixed grass prairie. From an appreciation of these qualities may grow a respect and concern for the environment. Whether or not there will be grasslands in the future, all depends upon you.

Acknowledgments

Writing this book has changed my life. I retired from my medical career in 1979 to seek knowledge in other fields and to broaden and diversify my life experience. All of these aims have been realized beyond my grandest expectations. But no one, least of all a writer, works in isolation, and any success I accrue from this publication is in part the result of the concern, encouragement, hospitality and aid offered by others.

The Explorations Program of the Canada Council was the first to endorse the project, and their generous funding enabled me to acquire essential field experience. Certainly the respected recommendations of magazine editors Arnet Sheppard and Gary W. Seib, on my behalf, were influential in obtaining the funding.

How can I begin to thank Francis and Myrna Walker and their children Trevor, Tracey and Twila who will never know how they lifted my spirits when I was lonely, and how their belief in me buoyed me when I was filled with self doubt? Their home was always mine, and I shall never forget. Others like Tom Donald and Mel Fitch gave me warmth, hospitality and friendship when I needed it most.

Research is a part of writing that I always enjoy, but the indefatigable efforts of the staff of the Main Library of the National Museums of Canada, especially Jean Guy Brisson, made the task easy as well.

To Aubrey I have dedicated this book, but that is so little to give to someone who has given me so much. Not only has she always been an effervescent companion, respected friend and a trusted confidant, but she has been a patient, constructive critic throughout.

Most of all I am indebted to the democratic system into which I was fortunate to be born. Without freedom of movement, freedom of speech and freedom of information my book could have been only a dream. I never forget the value of such freedoms, for on the day that I do, they will no longer be mine.

Additional Reading

Ammerman, A. J., 1975: Late Pleistocene population dynamics: An alternative view. Human Ecology, 3(4).

Anonymous, 1982: Management of saline soils. Agriculture Canada, Publication 1624/E.

Anonymous, 1978: Potash in Canada. Energy Mines and Resources, Government of Canada.

Anonymous, 1969: Saskatoon Wetlands Seminar. Canadian Wildlife Service, Report Series No. 6, Ottawa, 262pp.

Autenrieth, R., and E. Fichter, 1975: On the behavior and socialization of pronghorn fawns. Wildlife Monographs No. 42.

Babe, R., 1980: The mystery of migration. Macdonald & Jane's, London, 256pp.

Bambach, R., and A. M. Ziegler, 1980: Before Pangea: The geographies of the Paleozoic world. American Scientist 68(2).

Banfield, A. W. F., 1974: Mammals of Canada. University of Toronto Press, Toronto.

Barnes, R. D., 1980: Invertebrate zoology, 4th edition. Saunders College, Philadelphia, 1089pp.

Bartos, D. L., and P. L. Sims, 1974: Root dynamics of a shortgrass ecosystem. Journal of Range Management, Vol. 27(1), 33-36.

Beatty, C., 1975: Landscapes of southern Alberta — A regional geomorphology. University of Lethbridge Production Series, Lethbridge, 95pp.

Bekoff, M., 1980: The social ecology of coyotes. Scientific American, April.

Best, K. F., and J. Looman, 1971: Prairie grasses. Canada Agriculture, Publication No. 1413, 289pp.

Best K. F., and A. C. Best, 1969: Wild plants of the Canadian prairies. Canadian Department of Agriculture, Publication No. 983, 519pp.

Bielensten, H. U., 1980: Coal resources and reserves of Canada. Ministry of Supply and Services, Canada.

Bird, J. B., 1980: The natural landscapes of Canada, 2nd edition. John Wiley & Sons, Toronto, 260pp.

Blaker, A. A., 1976: Field photography — beginner and advanced technique. W. H. Freeman and Co., San Francisco, 451pp.

Borror, D. J., and R. E. White, 1970: A field guide to the insects of America north of Mexico. Houghton Mifflin Co., Boston, 404pp.

Braithwaite, M., 1970: The western plains. The Illustrated Natural History of Canada, Natural Science of Canada.

Bromley, P. T., and D. Kitchen, 1974: Courtship in the pronghorn Antilocapra americana. In The Behaviour of Ungulates and Its Relation to Management, IUCN Publication, New Series No. 24, Volume 1, 353-365.

Bryson, R., 1980: Ancient climes on the great plains. Natural History, July.

Budd, A. C., and J. B. Campbell, 1959: Flowering sequence of a local flora. Journal of Range Management, 12, 127-132.

Burt, W. H., 1976: A field guide to the mammals, 3rd edition. Houghton Mifflin Co., Boston, 340pp.

Burtt, E., 1981: Adaptiveness of animal colors. BioScience. November.

Carey, C., 1980: Ecology of avian incubation. BioScience 30 (2).

Carder, A. C., 1970: Climate and rangelands of Canada. Journal of Range Management, 23, 263-267.

Cody, M., 1981: Habitat selection in birds: roles of vegetation, structure, competitors and productivity. BioScience. February.

Coupland, R. T., and J. D. Dodd, 1966: Vegetation of saline areas in Saskatchewan. Ecology 47(6) 958-968.

Coupland R. T., and R. E. Johnson 1965: Rooting characteristics of native grassland species in Saskatchewan. Journal of Ecology 53, 475-507.

Coupland, R. T., and R. T. Brayshaw, 1953: The fescue grassland in Saskatchewan. Ecology 34(2) 386-405.

Coupland, R. T., 1950: Ecology of the mixed prairie in Canada. Ecological Monograph 20(4) 271-316.

Courtillot, V., and G. Vink, 1983: How continents break up. Scientific American. July.

Covey, C., 1984: The earth's orbit and ice ages. Scientific American, Vol. 250(2) 58-66.

Cox, A., and P. Coney, 1982: Growth of western North America. Scientific American, Vol. 247(5).

Cranna, M. D., 1973: Killdeer badlands — a prairie natural area. Blue Jay, 31(2) 68-77.

Crews, D., and W. Gartka, 1982: Ecological physiology of a garter snake. Scientific American, 247(5).

Curry-Lindahl, K., 1981: Wildlife of the prairies and plains. Harry N. Abrams Inc., New York, 232pp.

Dary, D., 1974: The buffalo book. Swallow Press Inc., Chicago, 374pp.

Denhardt, E. T., 1947: The horse of the Americas. University of Oklahoma Press, 286pp.

Dirschl, H. J., 1963: Food habits of pronghorn in Saskatchewan. Journal of Wildlife Management, 27(1) 81-93.

Dix, R. L., and R. G. Beidleman, 1969: The grassland ecosystem. Fort Collins, Colorado.

Duncan, P., 1979: Tallgrass prairie — the inland sea. The Lowell Press, Kansas City.

Eggleston, W., 1955: The short grass prairies of western Canada. Canadian Geographical Journal, 50 134-145.

England, R. E., 1969: Influence of animals on pristine conditions on the Canadian grasslands. Journal of Range Management, 22(2) 87-94.

Epp, H. T., 1968: Prehistoric human-bison ecology on the plains. Napao, 1 (1).

Epp, H. T., 1980: The great sand hills of Saskatchewan. A report for the Saskatchewan Department of the Environment. 156pp.

Fenton, M. B., 1983: Just bats. University of Toronto Press, Toronto. 165pp.

Fichter, E., 1974: On the bedding behaviour of pronghorn fawns. *In* The Behaviour of Ungulates and Its Relation to Management, IUCN Publication, New Series No. 24, Volume 1, 352-356.

Finnigan, J. T., 1982: Tipi rings and plains prehistory: a reassessment of their archeological potential. Archeological Survey of Canada, Mercury Series No. 108, National Museum of Canada, Ottawa, 295pp.

Finnigan, J. T., 1982: Tipi rings and plains prehistory: a reassessment of their archeological potential. National Museum of Canada, Mercury Series No. 108, 295pp.

Froom, B., 1972: The snakes of Canada. McClelland & Stewart Ltd., Toronto.

Gertsch, W. J., 1979: American spiders. 2nd edition. Van Nostrand Reinhold, Toronto, 274pp.

Goin, C. J., and O. Goin, and G. R. Zug, 1978: Introduction to herpetology, 3rd edition. W. H. Freeman & Co., San Francisco, 378pp.

Gordon, A., 1979: Geology of Saskatchewan: a historical approach. Western Extension College Education Publishers, Saskatoon, 67pp.

Gordon, B., 1979: Of men and herds in Canadian plains history. National Museum of Canada, Archeological Series No. 84.

Gray, J. K., 1967: Men against the desert. Western Producers Prairie Books, Saskatoon, 250pp.

Gunderson, H., 1978: Under and around a prairie dog town. Natural History, 87 (8).

Harrison, C., 1978: Nests, eggs and nestlings of North American birds. Collins, Toronto, 416pp.

Horridge, A., 1977: The compound eye of insects. Scientific American, April.

Hosie, R. C., 1979: Native trees of Canada, 8th edition. Fitzhenry & Whiteside Ltd., 380pp.

Hotchkiss, N., 1972: Common marsh, underwater and floating-leaved plants of the United States and Canada. Dover Publications Inc., New York, 124pp.

Houston, S., 1974: Abolished & forgotten national grasslands parks. Blue Jay, 32 (4) 204-209.

Jackson, R., and F. Raw, 1966: Life in the soil. Institute of Biology's Studies in Biology No. 2. Edward Arnold, London.

Jenness, D., 1977: The Indians of Canada, 7th edition. National Museum of Canada, Anthropology Series No. 15, 432pp.

Jensen, W., 1973: Fertilization in flowering plants. BioScience. January.

Johnsgard, P. A., 1973: Grouse and quails of North America. University of Nebraska Press, Lincoln.

Johnsgard, P. A., 1983: The grouse of the world. University of Nebraska Press, Lincoln, 413pp.

Johnston, A., 1970: A history of the rangelands of Western Canada. Journal of Range Management, Volume 23(1), 3-8.

Kehoe, T. F., 1976: Indian boulder effigies. Saskatchewan Museum of Natural History, Popular Series No. 12.

Kehoe, T. F., 1958: Tipi rings — the direct ethnological approach applied to an archeological problem. American Anthropology, 60(5) 861-873.

Keith, L. B., 1958: Some effects of increasing soil salinity on plant communities. Canadian Journal of Botany, 36, 79-89.

Kerr, R. A., 1983: Orbital variation — ice age link strengthened. Science, Vol. 219, January 21.

Kitchen, D. W., 1974: Social behavior and ecology of the pronghorn, Wildlife Monographs No. 38.

Klots, A. B., 1951: A field guide to the butterflies. Houghton Mifflin Co., Boston, 340pp.

Klots, E., 1966: The new field book of freshwater life. G. P. Putnam & Sons, New York.

Lang, A. H., 1970: Geology and Canada, 4th edition. Geological Survey of Canada. Ottawa, 32pp.

Langer, R. M., 1972: How grasses grow. Institute of Biology's Studies in Biology, No. 34, Edward Arnold, London.

Lent, P. C., 1974: Mother-infant relationships in ungulates. *In* The Behaviour of Ungulates and Its Relation to Management, IUCN Publications, New Series No. 24, Volume 1, 14-56.

Lofts, B., 1970: Animal photoperiodism. Institute of Biology's Studies in Biology, No. 25, Edward Arnold, London.

Looman, J., 1979: The vegetation of the Canadian prairie provinces — an overview. Phytocoenologia, 5(3) 347-366.

Looman, J., 1963: Preliminary classification of grasslands in Saskatchewan. Ecology, 44(1) 15-29.

Lord, J., 1982: Artful dodger (the hognose snake). Nature Canada, July/September.

Lott, D. F., 1974: Sexual and aggressive behaviour of American bison. In The Behaviour of Ungulates and Its Relation to Management, IUCN Publications, New Series No. 24, Volume 1, 382-395.

Lynch, W., 1983: Great balls of snakes. Natural History, April, 64-69.

Lynch, W., 1982: Prairie grasslands preserved in latest park. Canadian Geographic, February/March, 10-19.

Lynch, W., 1979: Prairie gypsy. Nature Canada, July/September, 9-11.

Lynch, W., 1977: Snakes. Blue Jay, 35(3).

Lynch, W., 1984: Horns and antlers. Canadian Geographic, August/September.

Malouf, C. L., 1961: Tipi rings of the high plains. American Antiquity 26(3) 381-389.

Martin, D. J., 1973: Selected aspects of burrowing owl ecology and behavior. Condor, 75, 446-456.

Maw, M. G., and M. M. Molloy, 1980: Prickly pear cactus on the Canadian plains. Blue Jay, 38(4).

Messick, J., and M. Hornocker, 1981: Ecology of the badger in southwestern Idaho. Wildlife Monographs, No. 76.

Milne, L., and M. Milne, 1978: Insects of the water surface. Scientific American, April.

Mitchell, G. J., 1980: The pronghorn antelope in Alberta. Alberta Department of Energy and Natural Resources. Edmonton, 165pp.

Mondor, C., 1976: The Canadian plains: the vanishing act. Nature Canada, 5(2), 32-40.

Morrison, H., 1969: A preliminary botanical review of the Big Muddy Valley of Saskatchewan. Blue Jay, 27(1), 45-53.

Mosquin, T. (Editor), 1976: Canada's threatened species and habitats. Canadian Nature Federation, Ottawa.

Muller, W., 1979: Botany — a functional approach, 4th edition. Macmillan Publishing Co., New York.

Munro, D., 1967: The prairies and the ducks. Canadian Geographical Journal, 45(1).

Murie, O. J., 1975: A field guide to animal tracks, 2nd edition. Houghton Mifflin Co., Boston, 375pp.

Mutch, R., 1970: Wildland fires and ecosystems — a hypothesis. Ecology, 51 (6) 1046-1051.

Nelson, J. G., 1973: The last refuge. Harvest House, Montreal, 230pp.

Newman, E., and P. Hartline, 1982: The infrared vision of snakes. Scientific American, March.

Patterson, F., 1982: Photography of natural things. Van Nostrand Reinhold, Toronto, 168pp.

Patterson, F., 1979: Photography and the art of seeing. Van Nostrand Reinhold, Toronto.

Patterson, F., 1977: Photography for the joy of it. Van Nostrand Reinhold, Toronto.

Peden, D. G., 1974: The trophic ecology of Bison bison on shortgrass plains. Journal of Applied Ecology, August, 489-497.

Pettigrew, J., and D. Presti, 1980: Ferromagnetic coupling to muscle receptors as a basis for geomagnetic field sensitivity in animals. Nature, Volume 285, May 8.

Platt, D. R., 1969: Natural history of the hognose snakes. University of Kansas, Publication of the Museum of Natural History, 18(4) 253-420.

Reeves, B. O. K., 1983: Six millenium of buffalo kills. Scientific American, September.

Reeves, B. O. K., 1983: Culture change in the northern plains: 1000 B.C. to A.D. 1000. Archeological Survey of Alberta, Occasional Paper No. 20, Alberta Culture, Edmonton, 390pp.

Renaud, W., 1980: The long billed curlew in Saskatchewan: status and distribution. Blue Jay, 38(4).

Ritchie, J. C., 1976: The late quaternary vegetational history of the western interior of Canada. Canadian Journal of Botany, 54(15) 1793-1818.

Russell, D., 1982: Mass extinction of the late Mesozoic. Scientific American, January.

Salt, W. R., and A. L. Wilk, 1966: Birds of Alberta. Queen's Printer, Ottawa, 511pp.

Sargeant, A. B., 1972: Movements and denning habits of a badger. Journal of Mammalogy, Volume 53(1), 207-210.

Schaller, F., 1968: Soil animals. University of Michigan Press, Ann Arbor.

Senecal, D., 1977: Coyote. Hinterland Who's Who Series, Canadian Wildlife Service, Ottawa.

Sheppard, D., 1979: Richardson ground squirrel. Hinterland Who's Who Series, Canadian Wildlife Service, Ottawa.

Sherbrooke, W. C., 1981: Horned lizards-unique reptiles of western North America. Southwest Parks and Monument Association, Arizona, 48pp.

Shmidt-Nielsen, K., 1979: Animal physiology: adaptation and environment, 2nd edition, Cambridge University Press, New York, 560pp.

Siever, R., et al,: 1983: The dynamic earth. Scientific American, 249(3) 46-189.

Sowls, L. K., 1955: Prairie ducks. Stickpole, Harrisburg, Pennsylvania 193pp.

Spry, I. M., 1963: The Palliser expediton — an account of John Palliser's British North American exploring expedition 1857-1860. Macmillan Co., Toronto.

Stearn, C., et al,: 1979: Geological evolution of North America, 3rd edition. John Wiley & Sons, Toronto, 566pp.

Stefferuck, A., (editor), 1948: Grass: yearbook of agriculture. U.S. Department of Agriculture, 446pp.

Stegner, W., 1966: Wolf willow. Viking Press, New York.

Swinton, W. E., 1974: Dinosaurs, 5th edition. British Museum Handbooks, London 47pp.

Terres, J. K., 1980: The Audubon society encyclopedia of North American birds. Alfred A. Knopf, New York, 1109pp.

Turner, A., 1955: How Saskatchewan dealt with the dust bowl. Geographical Magazine, Volume 28(4), 182-192.

Vance, F. R., and J. R. Jowsey, 1977: Wildflowers across the prairies. Western Producer Prairie Books, Saskatoon, 214pp.

Vaughan, T. A., 1978: Mammalogy, 2nd edition. W. B. Saunders, 522pp.

Vaughan, T. A., 1967: Food habits of the northern pocket gopher in shortgrass prairie. American Midland Naturalist, Volume 77, 176-189.

Verts, B. J., 1967: The biology of the striped skunk. University of Illinois Press, Chicago.

Wallmo, O . C., (Editor), 1981: Mule and black-tailed deer of North America. University of Nebraska Press, Lincoln.

Wedgewood, J., 1976: Burrowing owls. Blue Jay, 34(1).

Welty, J. C., 1975: Life of birds, 2nd edition. W. B. Saunders, Toronto.

Wiens, J. A., 1969: An approach to the study of ecological relationships among grassland birds. Ornithological Monographs No. 8 A.O.U.

Wilcox, S., 1972: Communication by surface waves. Journal of Comparative Physiology 80, 255-266.

Wiley, R. H., 1978: The lek mating system of the sage grouse. Scientific American, May.

Wilson, E. O., 1975: Sociobiology — the new synthesis. Cambridge, Massachusetts, Harvard University Press.

Woods, S. E., 1980: The squirrels of Canada. National Museum of Canada, Ottawa.

Wright, H., and A. Bailey, 1982: Fire ecology — U.S. and southern Canada. John Wiley & Sons, Toronto.

Yeaton, R. I., 1972: Social behavior and social organization in Richardson's ground squirrel in Saskatchewan. Journal of Mammalogy, 53, 139-149.